How to Assess Problem-Solving Skills in Math

by
Bena Kallick
and
Ross Brewer

NEW YORK • TORONTO • LONDON • AUCKLAND • SYDNEY

Cover design by Laurel Marx
Interior design by Solutions by Design, Inc.

ISBN 0-590-27051-6

Table of Contents

Preface

It was six o'clock in the morning. Ross and I were walking down a street in upstate New York. The morning was clear and the conversation exciting. We talked about the changing climate in education, about the "here to stayness" of portfolio assessment, which has flourished because teachers and students are its creators, and because it's a reform that is ultimately hand stitched in the classroom, not delivered from an ivory tower. We talked about the innovations in all curricular areas that have taken flight in the last decades, giving children today the opportunity to develop skills and knowledge through *purposeful* activities, such as hands-on science experiments, letter writing to favorite authors or local politicians, and keeping math journals, to name just a few. It could be a time for extraordinary opportunity, we believed, but only if teachers were given a voice in all of the instructional and assessment reforms. Without their contributions, teachers would end up being swamped with new curriculums and assessments that ignored the realities of their classrooms as well as the successful practices they were already using.

At the time, Ross and I both were working with schools, districts, and state education departments in the midst of changing assessment practices. Ross had been the architect of the Vermont portfolio assessment system. I had been consulting with schools, districts, and state departments regarding authentic assessment.We had begun to notice an inverse relationship: The farther an individual was from the classroom, the more certain he or she was about what should be expected of students! We saw the need to bring successful new teaching practices together with the new education standards. We also saw the potential of technology as a tool to facilitate that work.

By the time we had finished our walk, we had a plan. Because the National Council for Teachers of Mathematics (NCTM) had done outstanding work in setting new standards, we decided to focus on math assessments to reflect the standards. We would provide software and print material of rich and exciting work from classrooms that could serve as models for other teachers to use. No longer would each individual teacher have to work so hard to reinvent the wheel—they could draw from high-quality material already designed. A few months later, we formed a company—Exemplars—based on these principles:

- Teachers should not have to work alone.
- Teacher-developed and classroom-tested practices need to be shared.

The response to Exemplars assessment problems has been encouraging. Across the country, teachers have used them and adapted them to their classroom needs. When Terry Cooper of Scholastic Professional Books approached us to put our work into book form, we welcomed the opportunity, for the more teachers with whom we share the Exemplars problems, the closer we come to bridging the gap between broad educational reform movements and classroom practice.

—Bena Kallick

Introduction

"Teach to the test? How limiting! I never teach to the narrow way in which those tests are designed!" Many teachers we've worked with have made comments such as this; they feel constrained and even insulted by the one-dimensionality of the standardized test design, knowing their students are capable of much more than the test measures. They want to be able to assess students' knowledge in performance. They want to find reliable assessments that reflect the many dimensions of their math instruction.

Suppose there were a test worth teaching to? What would it look like, and how would you teach to make certain that students are given a fair and comfortable opportunity to perform? We hope the material in this book will help you begin to answer this question. The assessment problems in *How to Assess Problem-Solving Skills in Math* will give you a good start toward building a bank of math tasks that truly measure whether or not your students are becoming better problem solvers. In the chapters that follow, you will work with and revisit the problems, learning to use them...

- as tools to use when teaching the strategies of effective problem solving.
- as informal assessments that help you see what your students do and do not understand and what you need to reteach.

You'll also find information on...

- scoring students' work.
- developing your own problems to reflect the NCTM Standards.
- defining your role during assessments.
- setting up a classroom environment conducive to problem solving.
- using math portfolios to strengthen and showcase your students' problem-solving skills.

In the Appendix, you'll find ready-to-reproduce versions of the Exemplars problems as well as reproducible assessment rubrics to use and to share with students. You will also find samples of how other teachers have scored many of the problems. These will help you develop benchmark papers using your own students' work. (For additional background on teaching problem-solving, you may want to read Char Forsten's *Teaching Thinking and Problem Solving in Math* (Scholastic Professional Books, 1992) and Mark Illingworth's *Real-Life Math Problem Solving* (Scholastic Professional Books, 1996).

Why Do We Need to Cultivate Problem-Solving Skills?

The current "information age" requires our ability to not only take in information but also to make sense of it. We are constantly confronted by bar graphs, stock market percentages, measures of nutritional intake in our diet, machines that tell us our pulse rate to determine body conditioning, probabilities in weather maps, a sea of data on the Internet—and on and on! We need to be able to evaluate the data, recognize patterns, and learn how to abstract from patterns to determine trends of significance. In other words, we all need to be better problem solvers to manage information and make wise choices in our professional and personal lives.

Harnessing the Power of Children's Curiosity

When every other word a child says is *why*, he or she is like the world's greatest scientist and problem solver in miniature. In fact, young children take far more risks in solving problems than adults, for they often also ask, *Why not?* They have astounding perseverence, so great is their hunger to figure out how things work. As teachers, we need to bring a problem-solving approach to the curriculum in the earliest grades. We need to capitalize on children's natural curiosity about the world, and use it as a vehicle to teach them to think through challenges with imagination, determination, and reason.

We can tap into this curiosity by presenting math as a forum for solving problems as immediate and interesting as the challenges they tackle in the "off" hours, whether it's rationing their Halloween candy so it lasts until Thanksgiving, learning to toss a ball through a hoop, or calculating how old they will be when they might be allowed to stay up until midnight. Effective math teaching and math assessment is this simple: It's solving problems that stimulate children to generate ideas, collect and connect information, try out designs, invent, and use imagination and humor. Effective math teaching recognizes that problems in the real world are unstructured and that students therefore need to be taught how to *bring* structure to math challenges.

CHAPTER ONE

Authentic Assessment: What is It?

One of the defining characteristics of educators is that we often give a new name to ongoing work. Yet in so doing, we forget what we know. For example, we did a lot of work around core curriculum in the sixties and seventies and then renamed it "thematic" or "interdisciplinary" and somehow forgot that we were building on work that already existed. The same might be said for authentic assessment. In the early seventies, we had many "open" classrooms. At that time, teachers experimented with different forms of documentation of student work as it was produced through hands-on experiences, including narrative student self-evaluations, narrative teacher evaluations, performance evaluations, and conferences. We have returned to many of the practices—and many of the questions—that were explored in the seventies as if it were the first time we were asking those questions.

In our view, the essential questions about assessment continue to be:

- How can we collect credible information about students' learning when they are actively involved in the process of problem solving, reasoning, thinking, producing?
- How can we collect information regarding students' learning over time, rather than looking only at occasional snapshots?
- How can we report to parents and a broader public about student learning if the information is descriptive rather than reduced to singular scores?

Defining Our Terms

As we continue to refine our knowledge about assessments, we need to define our terms to make certain that we are not using new words for old concepts. Let us begin with the word *assessment*. What is assessment, and how is it different from evaluation?

Evaluation: Evaluation means to make a judgment, to place value on something. In the instance of education, we are making a judgment about student learning. In addition, we are making decisions about students on the basis of those judgments. For example, we decide whether students are gifted or remedial, whether they will pass or fail, or what group to place them in for the best performance.

Assessment: Assessments are tools for measuring. They serve as measures for making an evaluation. Traditionally, we have made judgments on the basis of one form of assessment: paper-and-pencil tests. When these tests are also standardized, we are making judgments on the basis of norm-referenced tests—often, a single snapshot of a student on a given day. As a result, we are measuring one of the most complex human events—learning—with a single and limited tool: paper-and-pencil, multiple-choice tests. Current research and practical knowledge have forced us to question the assumption that single measures are sufficient for making complex and significant judgments.

Furthermore, classroom teachers are concerned that a single measure does not adequately describe the performance of students on a day-to-day basis. Consequently, we now realize that no single tool for measuring should be used for making a judgment about human learning. In order to honor what we know about learning styles, brain research, situational applications of knowledge, and the distinction between book knowledge and practical applications of knowledge, we must develop multiple measures of assessment.

Think of a child you're teaching. If you want to know what he or she really understands about a concept you've taught, what do you do? What would you want to know? You might want to know whether the student is able to perform "on demand," meaning that he or she is able to respond to a set of problems that are presented in a test. You might also want to know how the student performs when in a group, working with others to solve a problem. In addition, you might want to see how the child is doing in relation to his or her previous work—i.e., is the child demonstrating growth and improvement across skill sets? Finally, you might want to know how the child feels about him- or herself as a mathematician; does the student exhibit confidence as a problem solver?

Now, think of a paper-and-pencil test. How much insight can such a test possibly give you about a child? A paper-and-pencil test has its place, of course, but it's not the whole picture.

Three Angles on Students' Progress

Many assessment experts believe that to make a wise judgment about a student we need to gather information from at least three angles of an assessment triangle (*see illustration below*). One angle might suggest how well a student performs on standardized or criterion-referenced measures; another might suggest how a student performs on the basis of his growth over time, as shown through the portfolio; and still another might suggest how well a student works on hands-on math performances requiring manipulatives. Some educators refer to this as triangulation; others talk about it as using multiple measures. Whatever you choose to call it, the important thing to remember is that when you document work from at least three perspectives, you have a better-informed method of making judgments for report cards, referrals, and parent conferences.

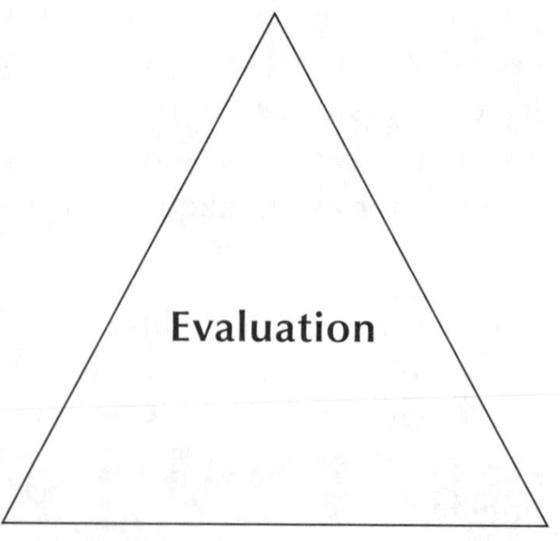

Authentic Assessment Shows Knowledge in Action

When we talk about authentic assessment, we mean demonstrations of learning through the application of knowledge in performance. The following list, adapted from Connecticut's Common Core of Learning, compares authentic tasks to traditional tasks:

ESSENTIAL VS. TANGENTIAL

- The task fits into the core curriculum.
- The learning task answers a question that teachers and students have, rather than simply serving as an exercise in operations. For example, have students grow plants and measure their growth; cook and use math applications to adapt a recipe; create bar graphs to represent book preferences among fifth graders; rearrange the room so that students can be in different groups when working on a project.

AUTHENTIC VS. CONTRIVED

- The task uses processes appropriate to the discipline.
- Students value the outcome of the task. For example, charting plant growth via a bar graph and comparing patterns of growth are appropriate to math and science and would be engaging—i.e, students would be invested in the outcome.

RICH VS. SUPERFICIAL

- The task leads to other problems.
- It raises other questions.
- It is "pregnant with possibilities." For example, once students have measured the growth of various kinds of plants, they might consider why there is a difference among plants. They might ask: Would orientation to the sun make a difference? More or less water? Would the results hold true over more than one experiment? What other plants might they graph to see if they could generalize about certain kinds of plants?

ENGAGING VS. UNINTERESTING

- The task is thought-provoking.
- It fosters persistence.

ACTIVE VS. PASSIVE

- The task puts students at center stage as workers, not as observers of a demonstration.
- It may require students to interact with one another.
- By doing the task, students construct meaning and deepen understanding.

Authentic Assessment = Authentic Learning

Thanks to the work of the NCTM, authentic assessment in mathematics is far ahead of other disciplines. The work of assessment reform has been guided by *The Curriculum and Evaluation Standards for School Mathematics*, which was published by the NCTM in 1989 to explain what it means to be mathematically literate in today's society and to create standards to guide the work of reforming curriculum and assessment.

According to the Standards, mathematics is much more than "concepts and skills to be mastered." It includes ways of investigating, reasoning, and communicating. Students should be self-confident in mathematics as a result of their experience in school.

> ***"Mathematical problem solving is nearly synonymous with doing mathematics."***
> —the NCTM Standards

The Standards lay out five goals for all students:

1 All students learn to **value** mathematics.

"Students...appreciate the role of mathematics in the development of our contemporary society and explore relationships among mathematics and the disciplines it serves: the physical and life sciences, the social sciences and the humanities."

2 All students become **confident** in their own ability to do mathematics.

"....students need to view themselves as capable of using their growing mathematical power to make sense of new problem situations in the world around them."

3 All students become mathematical **problem solvers.**

"The development of each student's ability to solve problems is essential if he or she is to be a productive citizen."

4 All students learn to **communicate** mathematically.

"...learning to use the signs, symbols and terms of mathematics. Students read, write and discuss ideas in which the use of the language of mathematics becomes natural. As students communicate their ideas, they learn to clarify, refine, and consolidate their thinking."

5 All students learn to **reason** mathematically.

"Making conjectures, gathering evidence, and building an argument to support such notions are fundamental to doing mathematics. In fact, a demonstration of good reasoning should be rewarded even more than students' ability to find correct answers."

In essence, the NCTM Standards stress one key concept: Problem solving is a necessary focus in mathematics. Although students need specific skills in order to solve problems (such as adding and subtracting), students become *mathematically literate* when they are actively applying those skills to a real-life problem. It is not enough for a second-grade student to know how to divide. She must know how to apply this skill "on the spot" when, for example, she's trying to figure out how many rides she can go on at the amusement park, given the amount of money she has in her pocket.

About the Problems in This Book

The problems we share in this book will help you move your students closer to independent mathematical thinking. They are based on the core idea of what it means to be a good problem solver. As you use them with your students, talk with them about the behaviors good problem solvers exhibit. This will help them identify these behaviors in themselves. Kathy Ernst, a first-grade teacher in Brattleboro, Vermont, defines an effective problem solver as follows:

A Good Problem Solver Is...

CURIOUS: Good problem solvers wonder about the world around them. They are interested in understanding why things work as they do.

PERSISTENT: Many times, solutions to good problems are not easily found. Good problem solvers stick to a problem until they have a solution. Having found one solution, they may well look for additional ones.

FLEXIBLE: Because problems are challenging, finding a solution may require that problem solvers explore alternative strategies, looking for an approach that might work or might work better than the one they first found.

RISK-TAKING: Sometimes solving problems means being wrong a few times before finding the solution; a good problem solver doesn't mind taking that chance.

REFLECTIVE: Effective problem solvers reflect on what they have learned from the problem-solving experience. The next time they tackle a problem, they benefit from this reflection.

These five characteristics reflect the NCTM standard regarding problem solving, which recommends that students be able to...

- use problem-solving approaches to investigate and understand mathematical content.
- formulate problems from everyday and mathematical situations.
- develop and apply strategies to solve a wide variety of problems.
- verify and interpret results with respect to the original problem.
- acquire confidence in using mathematics meaningfully.

(NCTM Standards/Grades K–4)

Good problem solvers...

- understand the challenge that the problem presents.
- use strategies to figure out the problem.
- use pictures and symbols to show how they solved the problem.

The Benefit of Using Uncued Problems

What makes the problems in this book different from the typical word problems you may find in many math textbooks is that they are *uncued.* Here is the difference between cued and uncued problems:

Cued Problems: When the student is presented with the problem, it follows the same pattern as many others that the student has practiced. For example, we often teach students to look for the key words in the problem. When it says *more than,* they know to add; when it says *less than*, they know to subtract. Unfortunately, when children go out into the world outside of school, no one offers them "key words."

Uncued Problems: The problems in this book ask the student, What do you do when you don't know what to do? This requires children's best thinking. There are no key words or traditionally set problems. The assessment information we gain from these problems helps us ask these questions of a student:

- How well do you understand the problem? Are you able to identify what the problem requires?
- Do you use strategies to help you solve the problem? Can you identify strategies you might try? Are you choosing the right operations for the problem?

- Can you show and explain your reasoning step by step? Are you beginning to use mathematical terms like *more than* and *less than* when you generate your results?
- Can you draw a picture of your problem, demonstrating your ability to think symbolically?

In short, the Exemplars approach tells you how a child is thinking—they give you more than a number on a page.

CHAPTER TWO

Using Exemplars Math Problems

In this chapter we'll present a sample performance task—Muffins—to show you how you may wish to introduce the Exemplars problems to your students.

Use Them as Instructional Tools Before Assessment

Terry Ferrarone, a Coordinator of Enrichment Programs for the Katonah-Lewisboro school district, in Katonah, New York, has been using the Exemplars problems with teachers and students for several years. Here, she shares what she's learned: "When we first introduced the Exemplars problems, the students cried, even the teachers cried! The children had been taught the skills and operations needed to do the tasks but not strategies and communication skills. So, unless your students have a comfort level with uncued problems, you will want to use the Exemplars performance tasks as an instructional tool before using them for formal assessment purposes."

Teach problem-solving strategies first: Before you present a problem to students, do it yourself. Figure out what skills and operations students will need to do the problem. Students need to use the strategies first. Two excellent resources are: George Lenchner's *Problem Solving in Mathematics* (Houghton Mifflin, 1983) and *The Problem Solver* (Creative Publications, 1987). "*The Problem Solver* has lessons that teach each strategy. The teachers and students I work with all love this book and couldn't do without it," says Terry. As you teach and practice the strategies and operations, the students become fluent problem solvers. Gradually move to problems requiring several steps.

Tackle a problem together: When your students are familiar with the strategies and are comfortable with problem solving, write an Exemplars problem on the chalkboard (*see Muffins sample on page 16*) and say to them, "Don't pick up a pencil. Let's talk about how we might do this; let's explore." Invite students to share their ideas. Give them a way to start the problem. From the outset, stress *how* to solve the problem as strongly as you stress finding the correct solution. Model this process of trying strategies and operations constantly.

Pair up for a practice run: Have students work in pairs to solve the problem. You may wish to review the four-step method with them first:

1. Understand the problem.

2. Plan how to solve it.
3. Carry out the plan.
4. Look back at your work.

Have an all-class discussion: When the class is ready, talk about how the partner teams attacked the problem. Invite students to come up to the board to show how they solved it. Ask questions such as: Does anyone have another way? Is one strategy better than another? We call this Math Seminar.

PROBLEM-SOLVING STRATEGIES

You might wish to post the following list in your classroom. Before students attack a problem, ask them: Can we use any of these to solve this problem?

- **Draw a picture of a diagram**
- **Find a pattern**
- **Make an organized list**
- **Make a table**
- **Solve a simpler problem**
- **Trial and error**
- **Experimenting**
- **Act out the problem**
- **Work backwards**
- **Write an equation**
- **Use deduction**

— from George Lenchner's *Problem Solving in Mathematics*

Muffins

Grade Level: K–2

THE TASK

Muffins cost 25 cents each. How many ways can you pay for the muffin? Please show and explain your work, using pictures, numbers, and words.

WHEN TO USE

Give this performance task *after* you teach a unit on money.

WHAT THIS TASK ACCOMPLISHES

It will identify students who have a conceptual understanding of coin recognition, value, and exchange properties.

CONCEPTS ASSESSED AND SKILLS DEVELOPED

- The problem-solving process
- Communication (diagram and/or verbal responses)
- Coin recognition
- Coin value
- Money counting
- Money exchange

WHAT STUDENTS WILL DO

Students will independently solve this problem on the task sheet given to them. If more room is needed, they may use the back and/or another sheet. Students may trace coins, if desired. They are encouraged to use diagrams, numbers, and words to indicate their mathematical thinking. There are many solutions to the problem. If children find more than one solution, they should show all they discover.

TEACHING TIPS

Ask yourself: What do the kids need to know (e.g., equivalencies of money, how to add and subtract)? Have I taught these skills?

Set the stage for this activity by talking about going to the store to buy a muffin. For example, "Today we'll pretend we're going to the store. We want to buy a muffin. Muffins cost 25 cents each. We have a lot of coins in our pockets and have to decide which coin or coins we want to use to pay for the muffin." Avoid modeling the problem or altering the task sheet.

POSSIBLE SOLUTIONS

1 quarter
2 dimes, 1 nickel
2 dimes, 5 pennies
1 dime, 2 nickels, 5 pennies
1 dime, 1 nickel, 10 pennies
1 dime, 15 pennies
5 nickels
4 nickels, 5 pennies
3 nickels, 10 pennies
2 nickels, 15 pennies
1 nickel, 20 pennies
25 pennies

Ten Steps for Teaching and Assessing With Exemplars Problems

1 Give each student a copy of a problem (see ready-to-use problems in the Appendix). Students will do their written work right on the page and on other sheets of paper, if necessary.

2 Read the directions aloud.

3 Have students work in pairs or alone to solve the problem. Students can use whatever manipulatives they want to help them.

4 As students work, take anecdotal notes. Record on self-stick notes whether students are using manipulatives, how they are using them, and any other information that helps you discern your students' thinking. If you are working with very young students who are not yet able to express their thinking in writing, then you can elicit their thinking by asking a series of questions. Careful, however, not to coach them too much.

5 Score their work using the Exemplars rubric shown below or the Exemplars student rubric shown on the next page. (See the Appendix for reproducible versions; see Chapter 3 for a more detailed discussion of scoring.)

EXEMPLARS RUBRIC

Level	Understanding	Strategies, Reasoning, Procedures	Communication
Novice	• There is no solution, or the solution has no relationship to the task. • Inappropriate concepts or procedures are used.	• No evidence of a strategy or procedure, or uses a strategy that does not help solve the problem. • No evidence of mathematical reasoning. • There were so many errors in mathematical procedure that the problem could not be solved.	• There is no explanation of the solution, the explanation cannot be understood or it is unrelated to the problem. • There is no use or inappropriate use of mathematical representations (e.g., figures, diagrams, graphs, tables, etc.) • There is no use, or mostly inappropriate use, of mathematical terminology and notation.
Apprentice	• The solution is not complete, indicating that parts of the problem are not understood.	• Uses a strategy that is partially useful, leading some way toward a solution, but not to a full solution of the problem. • Some evidence of mathematical reasoning. • Could not completely carry out mathematical procedures.	• There is an incomplete explanation; it may not be clearly presented. • There is some use of appropriate mathematical representation. • There is some use of mathematical terminology and notation appropriate to the problem.
Practitioner	• The solution shows that the student has a broad understanding of the problem and the major concepts necessary for its solution.	• Uses a strategy that leads to a solution of the problem. • Uses effective mathematical reasoning. • Mathematical procedures used appropriately.	• There is a clear explanation. • There is appropriate use of accurate mathematical representation. • There is effective use of mathematical terminology and notation.
Expert	• The solution shows a deep understanding of the problem, including the ability to identify the appropriate mathematical concepts and the information necessary for its solution.	• Uses a very efficient and sophisticated strategy leading directly to a solution. • Employs refined and complex reasoning. • Applies procedures accurately to correctly solve the problem and verify the results.	• There is a clear, effective explanation detailing how the problem is solved. All of the steps are included so that the reader does not need to infer how and why decisions were made. • Mathematical representation is actively used as a means of communicating ideas related to the solution of the problem. • There is precise and appropriate use of mathematical terminology and notation.

6 Hand back work to each student, with the filled-out student rubric stapled to the problem sheet. Take a moment to ask each student questions like: What do you think you need to work on? Encourage them with written or verbal comments such as: This is a nicely explained piece. The rubric is powerful—it helps demystify the problem-solving process for children and shows them step-by-step the path

MATH STUDENT RUBRIC			
Level	**Understanding**	**Strategies, Reasoning, Procedures**	**Communication**
Novice	I do not understand the problem.	I am not sure how to do it.	I have no explanation. I'm not sure how to draw the problem, or which numbers to use.
Apprentice	I think I understand the problem.	I got started. I'm still thinking. I have part of the answer. It would help me to work with somebody.	I can explain some of what I did. I tried to use pictures, numbers, graphs, or words. My answer might be right.
Practitioner	I got it! I understand the problem.	I used a plan to solve the problem.	I can tell you or show you how I got the answer. I used mathematical terms and models, pictures, graphs, or numbers to explain how I did the problem. You can see how I did it.
Expert	I got it! I can prove to you that I'm right. I know I'm right.	I can show you several plans to solve this problem. I can prove to you that my answer is right.	I very clearly laid out step by step how I solved the problem. I used words, pictures, numbers, models, or graphs to show exactly how I did the problem, and proved that my answer is right. I can even show you another way to do the problem.

Students can use the student rubric to evaluate their own work. Often this helps the students to set goals for themselves. As students become better evaluators, thier work improves measurably.

to a good performance. Most important, sharing rubrics with students helps them to set goals for themselves, because they now have such a concrete picture of what they need to work on.

7 Next, talk as a class about the problem they have just done. Put student volunteers' work on the overhead, or invite children to come to the board to show how they did the problem. Ideally, when you create a trusting environment, children will feel free to go to the board and say, "I got this far, and then I got stuck. Now what should I have done?" At this point, children can take turns helping him/her through the task. Point out how someone was right, how someone was wrong. Use manipulatives to demonstrate.

8 After you score your class's work, and if you see a lot of students have made a similar mistake, gather those students and do a mini-lesson on this skill. Children are often unfamiliar with the communication end of problem solving; they're not used to writing about math. You may have to do several all-class mini-lessons on how to explain the process. Having children keep math journals will help sharpen their communication skills.

9 Do a couple of Exemplars problems each week. Using the guidelines outlined in Chapter 4, develop multistep problems of your own.

10 Have whole-class discussions about the qualities of the various performance levels, using samples of students' work at each level—these are called benchmark papers. Put them on the overhead, or make copies. This encourages students to assess work for themselves.

On the next page, you will find samples of student work on the Muffins Problem.

EXEMPLARS RUBRIC			
Level	**Understanding**	**Strategies, Reasoning, Procedures**	**Communication**
Novice	• There is no solution, or the solution has no relationship to the task. • Inappropriate concepts or procedures are used.	• No evidence of a strategy or procedure, or uses a strategy that does not help solve the problem. • No evidence of mathematical reasoning. • There were so many errors in mathematical procedure that the problem could not be solved.	• There is no explanation of the solution, the explanation cannot be understood or it is unrelated to the problem. • There is no use or inappropriate use of mathematical representations (e.g., figures, diagrams, graphs, tables, etc.) • There is no use, or mostly inappropriate use, of mathematical terminology and notation.
Apprentice	• The solution is not complete, indicating that parts of the problem are not understood.	• Uses a strategy that is partially useful, leading some way toward a solution, but not to a full solution of the problem. • Some evidence of mathematical reasoning. • Could not completely carry out mathematical procedures.	• There is an incomplete explanation; it may not be clearly presented. • There is some use of appropriate mathematical representation. • There is some use of mathematical termi and notation appropriate to the problem
Practitioner	• The solution shows that the student has a broad understanding of the problem and the major concepts necessary for its solution.	• Uses a strategy that leads to a solution of the problem. • Uses effective mathematical reasoning. • Mathematical procedures used appropriately.	• There is a clear explanation. • There is appropriate use of accurate mat representation. • There is effective use of mathematical te and notation.
Expert	• The solution shows a deep understanding of the problem, including the ability to identify the appropriate mathematical concepts and the information necessary for its solution.	• Uses a very efficient and sophisticated strategy leading directly to a solution. • Employs refined and complex reasoning. • Applies procedures accurately to correctly solve the problem and verify the results.	• There is a clear, effective explanation de how the problem is solved. All of the ste included so that the reader does not nee how and why decisions were made. • Mathematical representation is actively means of communicating ideas related t solution of the problem. • There is precise and appropriate use of mathematical terminology and notation.

Unlike the student rubrics—which are used to guide instruction but don't "count" in children's grades—these rubrics are used for formal assessments, which you might give four times a year. For more about formal assessments, see Chapter 5. For a reproducible version of the Exemplars rubric, see page 125.

EXEMPLARS RUBRIC			
Level	**Understanding**	**Strategies, Reasoning, Procedures**	**Communication**
Novice	• There is no solution, or the solution has no relationship to the task. • Inappropriate concepts or procedures are used.	• No evidence of a strategy or procedure, or uses a strategy that does not help solve the problem. • No evidence of mathematical reasoning. • There were so many errors in mathematical procedure that the problem could not be solved.	• There is no explanation of the solution, the explanation cannot be understood or it is unrelated to the problem. • There is no use or inappropriate use of mathematical representations (e.g., figur diagrams, graphs, tables, etc.) • There is no use, or mostly inappropriate mathematical terminology and notation.
Apprentice	• The solution is not complete, indicating that parts of the problem are not understood.	• Uses a strategy that is partially useful, leading some way toward a solution, but not to a full solution of the problem. • Some evidence of mathematical reasoning. • Could not completely carry out mathematical procedures.	• There is an incomplete explanation; it m clearly presented. • There is some use of appropriate mather representation. • There is some use of mathematical termi and notation appropriate to the problem
Practitioner	• The solution shows that the student has a broad understanding of the problem and the major concepts necessary for its solution.	• Uses a strategy that leads to a solution of the problem. • Uses effective mathematical reasoning. • Mathematical procedures used appropriately.	• There is a clear explanation. • There is appropriate use of accurate mat representation. • There is effective use of mathematical te and notation.
Expert	• The solution shows a deep understanding of the problem, including the ability to identify the appropriate mathematical concepts and the information necessary for its solution.	• Uses a very efficient and sophisticated strategy leading directly to a solution. • Employs refined and complex reasoning. • Applies procedures accurately to correctly solve the problem and verify the results.	• There is a clear, effective explanation de how the problem is solved. All of the ste included so that the reader does not nee how and why decisions were made. • Mathematical representation is actively means of communicating ideas related t solution of the problem. • There is precise and appropriate use of mathematical terminology and notation.

Name Apprentice Date

Muffins

Muffins cost 25¢. How many ways can you pay for the muffin? Please show and explain your work using pictures, numbers, and words.

Name **Practitioner** Date

Muffins

Muffins cost 25¢. How many ways can you pay for the muffin? Please show and explain your work using pictures, numbers, and words.

EXEMPLARS RUBRIC

Level	Understanding	Strategies, Reasoning, Procedures	Communication
Novice	• There is no solution, or the solution has no relationship to the task. • Inappropriate concepts or procedures are used.	• No evidence of a strategy or procedure, or uses a strategy that does not help solve the problem. • No evidence of mathematical reasoning. • There were so many errors in mathematical procedure that the problem could not be solved.	• There is no explanation of the solution, t explanation can not be understood or it i unrelated to the problem. • There is no use or inappropriate use of mathematical representations (e.g., figure diagrams, graphs, tables, etc.) • There is no use, or mostly inappropriate mathematical terminology and notation.
Apprentice	• The solution is not complete indicating that parts of the problem are not understood.	• Uses a strategy that is partially useful, leading some way toward a solution, but not to a full solution of the problem. • Some evidence of mathematical reasoning. • Could not completely carry out mathematical procedures.	• There is an incomplete explanation; it m clearly presented. • There is some use of appropriate mathem representation. • There is some use of mathematical termi and notation appropriate to the problem.
(Practitioner)	• The solution shows that the student has a broad understanding of the problem and the major concepts necessary for its solution.	✓ Uses a strategy that leads to a solution of the problem. ✓ Uses effective mathematical reasoning. ✓ Mathematical procedures used appropriately.	✓ There is a clear explanation. • There is appropriate use of accurate math representation. ✓ There is effective use of mathematical te and notation.
Expert	✓ The solution shows a deep understanding of the problem, including the ability to identify the appropriate mathematical concepts and the information necessary for its solution.	• Uses a very efficient and sophisticated strategy leading directly to a solution. • Employs refined and complex reasoning. • Applies procedures accurately to correctly solve the problem and verify the results.	• There is a clear, effective explanation de how the problem is solved. All of the ste included so that the reader does not nee how and why decisions were made. ✓ Mathematical representation is actively u means of communication ideas related t solution of the problem. • There is precise and appropriate use of mathematical terminology and notation.

A Practitioner may be able to clearly identify many solutions to this task, but it may appear in a more random order. The Expert will clearly show some organization in his/her solution to be sure nearly all possible combinations of coins are used.

Name **Expert** Date

Muffins

Muffins cost 25¢. How many ways can you pay for the muffin? Please show and explain your work using pictures, numbers, and words.

EXEMPLARS RUBRIC

Level	Understanding	Strategies, Reasoning, Procedures	Communication
Novice	• There is no solution, or the solution has no relationship to the task. • Inappropriate concepts or procedures are used.	• No evidence of a strategy or procedure, or uses a strategy that does not help solve the problem. • No evidence of mathematical reasoning. • There were so many errors in mathematical procedure that the problem could not be solved.	• There is no explanation of the solution, tl explanation cannot be understood or it is unrelated to the problem. • There is no use or inappropriate use of mathematical representations (e.g., figure diagrams, graphs, tables, etc.) • There is no use, or mostly inappropriate mathematical terminology and notation.
Apprentice	• The solution is not complete, indicating that parts of the problem are not understood.	• Uses a strategy that is partially useful, leading some way toward a solution, but not to a full solution of the problem. • Some evidence of mathematical reasoning. • Could not completely carry out mathematical procedures.	• There is an incomplete explanation; it ma clearly presented. • There is some use of appropriate mathem representation. • There is some use of mathematical termi and notation appropriate to the problem.
Practitioner	• The solution shows that the student has a broad understanding of the problem and the major concepts necessary for its solution.	• Uses a strategy that leads to a solution of the problem. • Uses effective mathematical reasoning. • Mathematical procedures used appropriately.	• There is a clear explanation. • There is appropriate use of accurate math representation. • There is effective use of mathematical terminology and notation.
(Expert)	✓ The solution shows a deep understanding of the problem, including the ability to identify the appropriate mathematical concepts and the information necessary for its solution.	✓ Uses a very efficient and sophisticated strategy leading directly to a solution. ✓ Employs refined and complex reasoning. • Applies procedures accurately to correctly solve the problem and verify the results.	• There is a clear, effective explanation detailing how the problem is solved. All of the steps are included so that the reader does not need to infer how and why decisions were made. ✓ Mathematical representation is actively used as a means of communicating ideas related to the solution of the problem. • There is precise and appropriate use of mathematical terminology and notation.

20 Problems to Use

You'll find more great math tasks—plus teaching tips and scored student work samples—in the Appendix. The chart below will give you a quick look at what's there. Use the steps outlined in this chapter to introduce the problems to your students.

THE PROBLEM	WHEN TO USE
Muffins	money, addition
Kite Shop	collecting, organizing information, shapes
Farmyard	addition
Field Trip	addition, patterns
Flags	patterns, combinations, reasoning
In Line	reasoning, organizing information
Pentomino	estimation, shapes, geometry
Six-Pack of Soda	counting, grouping, or patterns
Darts	addition
Bowls of Apples	fractions and division
Tollbooth	money, addition, counting
Sink or Float	comparison, estimation, patterns
7 Coins	money
The Fish Dilemma	addition, combinations
Witches' Troubles	addition, combinations
Shoe Graph	measurement, collecting and organizing information
Hamsters	computation, whole numbers
Pizza Party	patterns, whole numbers, fractions, geometry
Clay Pots	addition
Reading for Mom	addition

CHAPTER THREE

Scoring Students' Work

In this chapter, we'll take a closer look at how to score students' work on the Exemplars problems in a way that...

- constructively informs the students about their performances and how they might improve.
- informs the instructional decisions that you make.
- informs parents about their children's progress and support they can provide.

The Thinking Behind The Score

The main idea to keep in mind as you work with the Exemplars scoring rubric—or develop scoring criteria of your own—is that assessment can serve as valuable information *without sorting or classifying students*. When assessment is seen from this perspective, it encourages students to see themselves as learners, realizing that acquiring knowledge often leads to valleys before arriving at new peaks.

This is true for adults as well as children. Think about the first time you tried to use a word processor. First, you tried reading a manual that seemed unintelligible because there was a whole new vocabulary, a new set of commands and options, and menus that you did not immediately understand. When you were finally able to write what you set out to write, what would normally take one hour might easily have taken three. Nonetheless, it was worth the effort.

Whether by persistence, confidence that you could learn, or encouragement from someone else, you persevered rather than fall back on the electric typewriter. Finally, after personal mastery, you may have made two observations: (1) writing on a word processer is, indeed, more efficient and effective than on a typewriter; (2) using the word processor has changed the way you now think about writing.

The same process of struggle and mastery applies to a student as he or she becomes a mathematical problem solver. When problem-solving strategies become a learned way of facing situations of uncertainty, the student will not only be more efficient and effective as a problem solver but also will have a different way of thinking about problem solving. What we're after, then, are assessment criteria that keep these peaks and valleys and changes in perspective in mind.

Rubrics That Describe Growth Over Time

When learning is described on a continuum, it reinforces different entry points for learning without suggesting embarrassment or inadequacy. We need to think about a developmental continuum that describes learning from two perspectives:

1. What is the developmental stage the learner is in on the continuum? How close is the learner to personal mastery or expertise?
2. What is the quality of the work the learner produces at that stage? Our goal is to offer sufficient descriptive feedback for a learner so that he or she can set personal goals.

Rubrics serve to describe the basis upon which you would make a judgment about performance. When the rubrics are linked to the NCTM Standards, they help us describe where students are on a continuum of progress toward meeting the standards. The Exemplars rubric, based on the NCTM Standards, defines the important factors in assessing problem solving.

The Exemplars Rubric

The Exemplars rubric defines four levels of student performance:

The Novice really can't get started. This child does not have an appropriate solution to the problem because he does not understand the problem, can't develop a strategy, and/or can't carry out the mathematics procedures that are necessary for its solution. The Novice does not have an explanation that can be understood or is related to the problem. He either does not use mathematics figures, terminology, or notation at all, or uses them inappropriately.

The Apprentice is able to get started but can't completely solve the problem. The Apprentice understands enough of the problem and is able to develop a partial strategy to begin but does not have enough understanding to reach a full solution. There is some use of appropriate mathematical terminology, notation, or representation.

The Practitioner understands the problem well and chooses a suitable strategy that leads him to solve the problem correctly. He uses mathematical reasoning and mathematical procedures effectively. His explanation is clear, and there is appropriate use of mathematical representation, notation, and terminology.

The Expert solution goes beyond the Practitioner's. The Expert employs a more efficient and sophisticated strategy and uses more refined and complex reasoning. She applies procedures accurately and correctly. Her explanation is clear, requiring no inference on the part of the reader. She uses mathematical representation to actively communicate, and terminology and notation precisely and appropriately. She can verify her solutions by checking step-by-step.

When you assess your students' work, you will apply these four levels of performance to the following three phases of successful problem solving:

Understanding: How well did the student understand the problem?

Strategies, Reasoning, and Procedures: What strategies did the student use in solving the problem? Is there evidence of mathematical reasoning? Did the child make an appropriate application of mathematics procedures when solving the problem?

Communication: How well did the student explain her solution? How well did she communicate mathematical representation, terminology, and notation?

A Student Can Be a Novice in One Area, an Expert in Another

It is possible that sometimes you will have students who might be a Practitioner in understanding the problem and in the choice of strategies but an Apprentice in communication. You might want to note these independently, as this would draw attention to the need for the student to work on her communication skills. Or you might want to score the results as a single score. If you do, you can make your own overall assessment—the student really is working at a Practitioner level. You might average the levels of performance and come to the conclusion that the student is a Practitioner. Whatever you do, it is important for the student to know that she needs to continue to improve her communication skills.

What to Expect

Aim to get the whole class to the Practioner level. Generally speaking, you will have very few Novices or Experts—most students will fall in the Apprentice and Practitioner levels. Some tasks are very elementary, and you won't have any Novices. If you have lots of Experts, it might be that the problem is not as rigorous as it should be.

Sharing the Scoring Rubric With Students

Fortunately, or unfortunately, we will not be able to go with our students into the world beyond school. They may internalize our voices reminding them to check for accuracy, to remember that neatness counts, and to stay organized. However, we must build those internal voices into habits of the mind—the discipline to persist with a problem in the face of uncertainty, knowing they need to check for accuracy and precision, caring about the quality of the work they turn in. For more information on specific habits of the mind, read *What Human Beings Do When They Behave Intelligently and How They Can Become More So* by Arthur Costa (ASCD).

Continually sharing with children the characteristics of good work is one of the best ways to build these habits of mind. There are many ways to do this, from impromptu conversations about good work, to student-generated wall charts of What Makes a Piece of Work Good, to sharing more formal rubrics with students. Continually encourage children to set goals, asking individual students and the class such questions as: Where are we? Where do we go from here?

To begin, talk about what we mean when we say, "understands the problem." You might say, "What would I see and hear that would tell me you understand the problem?" As the students develop a language for what you would like to see and hear, you can transform the indicators in the rubric into their language. They can even score themselves before they turn in their work. The more experience they have with self-scoring and scoring the work of the group, the better they will become at developing quality performances.

Practice Scoring

Practice at scoring will make the process easier and improve your consistency. It might be useful to begin by working in teams with your colleagues to look at student work.

Here is an exercise that will help you to look at your student work. It is designed to focus assessment on what we actually *see* in the students' work, not on what is missing. It is based on the understanding that description is a first necessary step for good evaluation. Pass around one student's work—either an Exemplars problem or one of your own. Each person comments, describing something they see in the work. For example, "I see that he is adding"; "I see that he is using two-digit numbers." Keep passing the paper around until everyone feels there is nothing more to say. In a group of five or six (optimal size), the paper may be passed around three times. Don't stop until you have exhausted the work.

Description is the first step toward evaluation. The next is interpretation. Here you ask, How do I make sense out of what I have described? What inferences or implications do I see for the student as I read the work?

Finally, there is evaluation. What judgment do I make regarding the work? Using the Exemplars rubric, ask: Is this student a Novice? Why do I say that? Is this student a Practitioner? What do I see in the work that tells me that?

This process will lead you and your colleagues to interesting insights and discussions about your students and their mathematics.

Using Benchmark Papers

In assessing student work, it helps to select benchmark papers—examples of previously scored student work— at each level of performance. This will make your assessment more efficient and more consistent. Be sure to check your benchmark papers—make sure they're correct! Use the rubric on page 125, and add any additional description specific to the task at hand.

Kite Shop: A Practice Problem

Now it's your turn. On the pages that follow, you'll find four students' work from the Exemplars problem Kite Shop. Go through the process we outlined earlier to determine which work should be rated Novice, Apprentice, Practitioner, and Expert.

- First, describe what you see in each piece of work.
- Next, interpret what you have described. Ask yourself if the student is solving the problem that was posed. If not, what problem is he solving? Are his procedures appropriate? Is his strategy a workable one? What evidence is there of mathematical reasoning? Is there mathematical communication? How well does he communicate his thinking?
- Finally, evaluate. Would you say that the student is a Novice, Apprentice, Practitioner, or Expert?

Work on this with your colleagues. Where do you disagree ? Discuss with your colleagues what you see that they don't or what they see that you don't. What is it in the piece of work that led you to evaluate it one way and your colleague(s) another. How often do you disagree?

We have included scored versions of students' work on Kite Shop on page 70 in the Appendix. Also in the Appendix are other scored student samples from other Exemplars problems.

Kite Shop

Grade Level: K-2

THE TASK

Spring is a time to look for a kite to catch the wind. Look at the kite shapes, and use your pattern blocks to fill them. You need to find different solutions for each kite. Write a math sentence, and make a chart or graph for each kite you fill in.

WHEN TO USE

After teaching about pattern blocks and geometric shapes. Tie in to a springtime exploration of kite flying.

WHAT THIS TASK ACCOMPLISHES

It provides an opportunity for students to find more than one solution, to practice using their spatial sense, and to practice creating math sentences and representations.

CONCEPTS ASSESSED AND SKILLS DEVELOPED

- **Geometry and spatial sense:** modeling, drawing, and describing geometric ideas
- **Statistics and probability:** collecting, organizing, and describing data; interpreting displays of data
- **Whole number computation:** selecting and using computational techniques appropriate to the specific problem
- **Problem solving:** using problem-solving approaches to investigate and understand mathematical content; relating problems to everyday situations
- **Communication:** relating physical materials to mathematical concepts; reflecting on and clarifying thinking about mathematical situations
- **Reasoning:** justifying answers and solution processes; drawing logical conclusions about mathematical situations
- **Connections:** applying mathematical thinking to solve problems in other disciplines, such as science, social studies, and art

WHAT STUDENTS WILL DO

Students will utilize their visual and spatial skills to fill in the different kite shapes in more than one way. The students will use pattern blocks to explore different solutions and then choose two for each shape to record. They will provide a math sentence for each solution and then chart or graph their designs in a logical format. Finally, they will color in their favorite kite design. Later, they will use these designs for a class sorting and graphing activity.

TIME REQUIRED FOR THE TASK

60 minutes

TEACHING TIPS

Put the following 3 kite shapes on a sheet for each student, drawing them so that pattern blocks fit inside them.

Read Gail Gibbon's beautifully illustrated *Catch the Wind!* to spark discussions about kite designs. Discuss the correct names for the different pattern blocks and their attributes.

Prior to doing the problem, students will need a variety of opportunities to practice using their visual and spatial skills, using pattern blocks, pentominoes, and tangrams. Students will also need many opportunities to write math sentences and use graphing skills.

SUGGESTED MATERIALS

- Literature that illustrates a variety of kite shapes
- Pattern blocks for small groups
- Sheet with 3 different kite shapes to fill in

with pattern blocks for each student

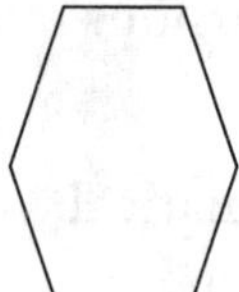

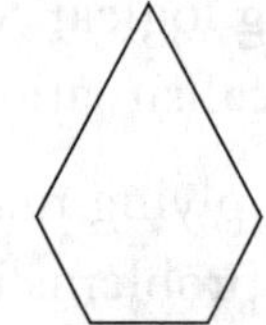

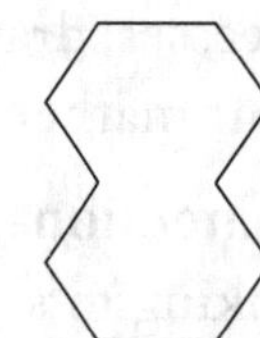

- Pencils, colored pencils, or crayons
- Graph paper (optional)

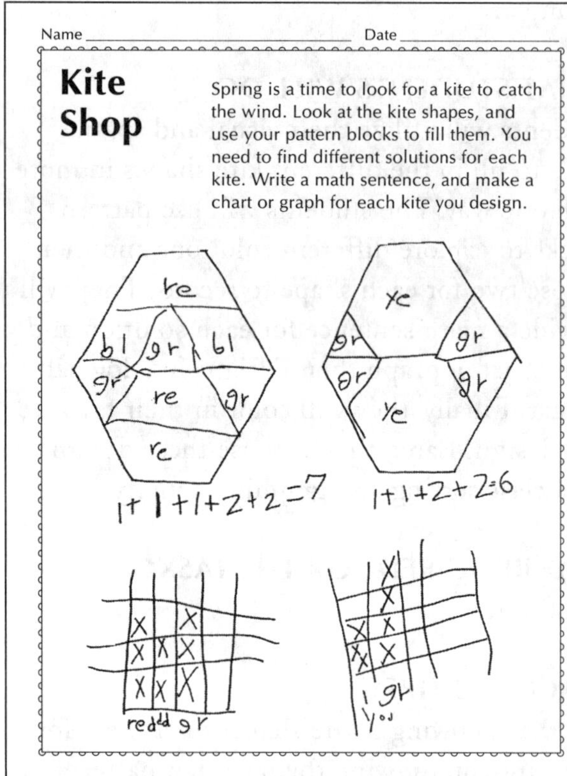

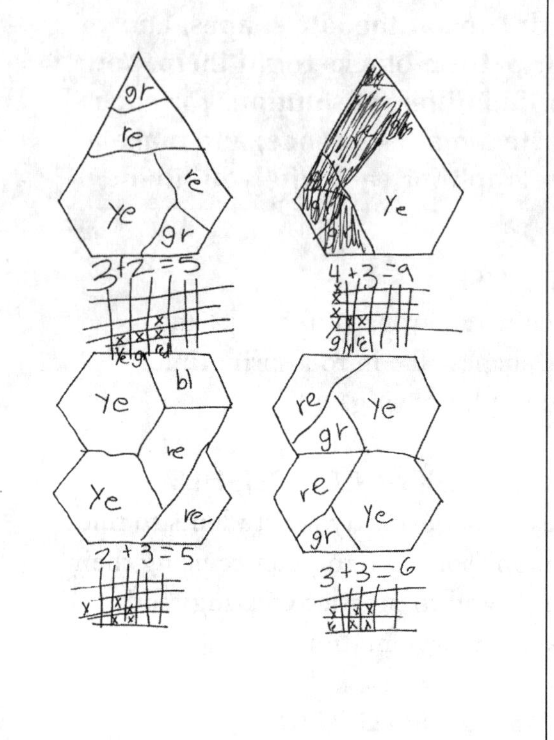

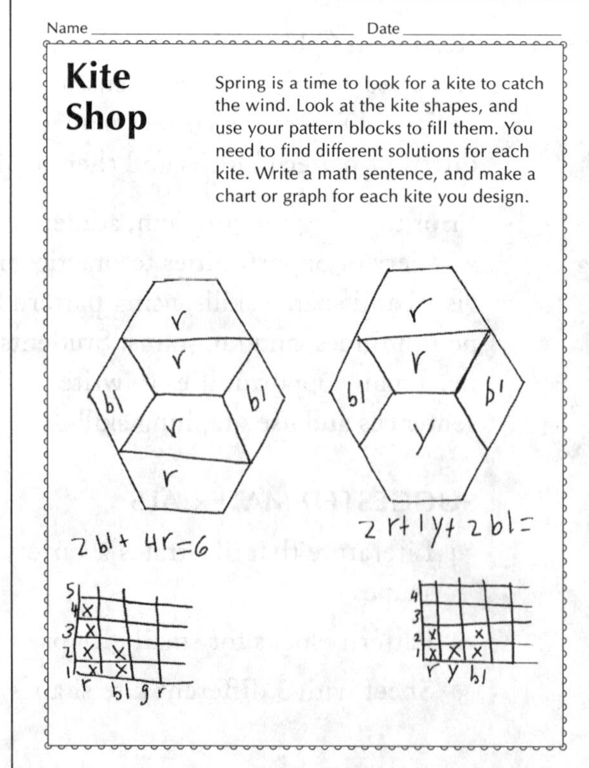

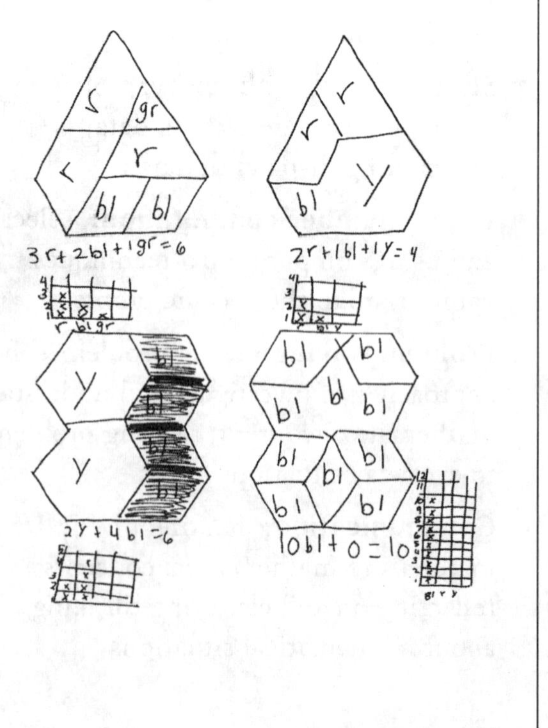

POSSIBLE SOLUTIONS

This task lends itself to several possible solutions for each kite shape. In their solutions, the blocks must be labeled by color, and children must include an appropriate mathematical sentence for each design, as well as a graph or chart to show their interpretation of data. Some students might chart each design or combine some of them, which would illustrate extensions of mathematical ideas.

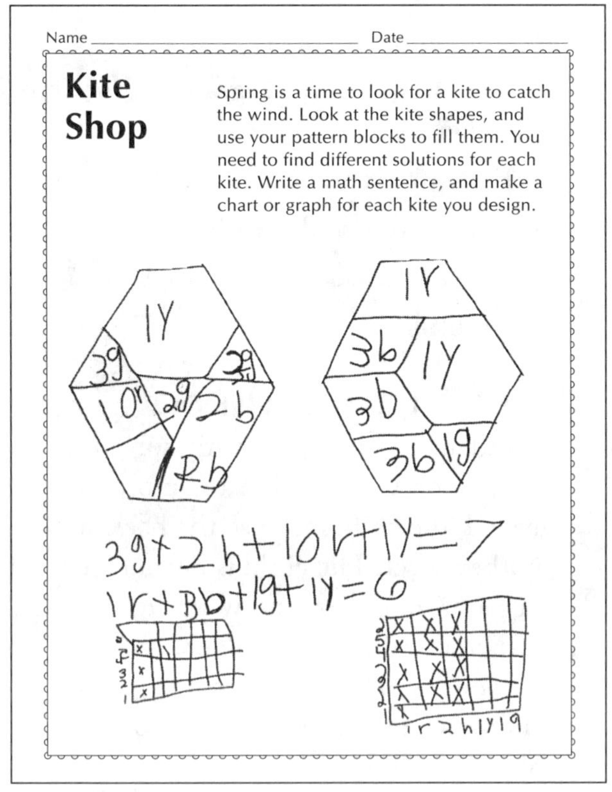
Name ______________________ Date ______________

Kite Shop

Spring is a time to look for a kite to catch the wind. Look at the kite shapes, and use your pattern blocks to fill them. You need to find different solutions for each kite. Write a math sentence, and make a chart or graph for each kite you design.

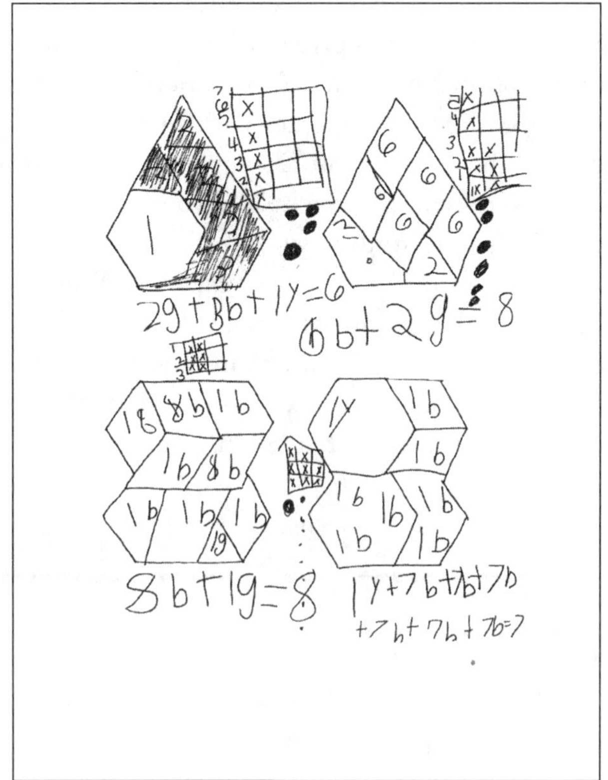

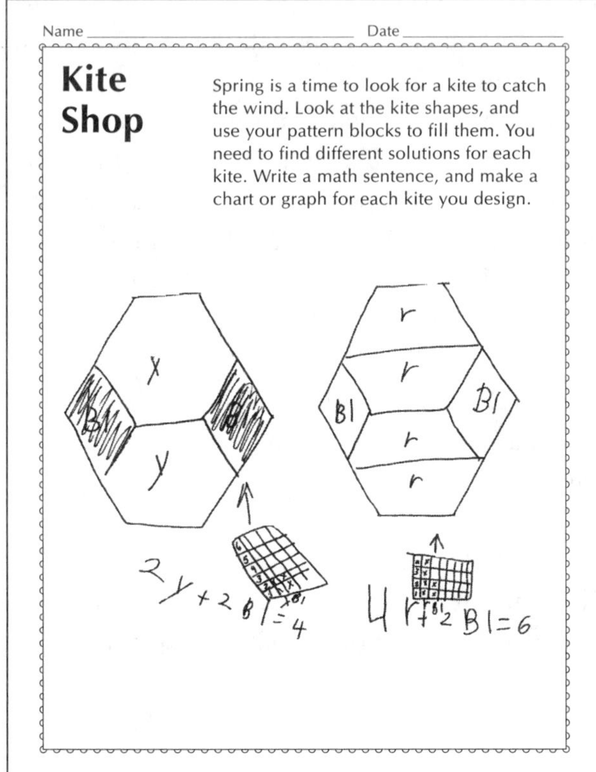
Name ______________________ Date ______________

Kite Shop

Spring is a time to look for a kite to catch the wind. Look at the kite shapes, and use your pattern blocks to fill them. You need to find different solutions for each kite. Write a math sentence, and make a chart or graph for each kite you design.

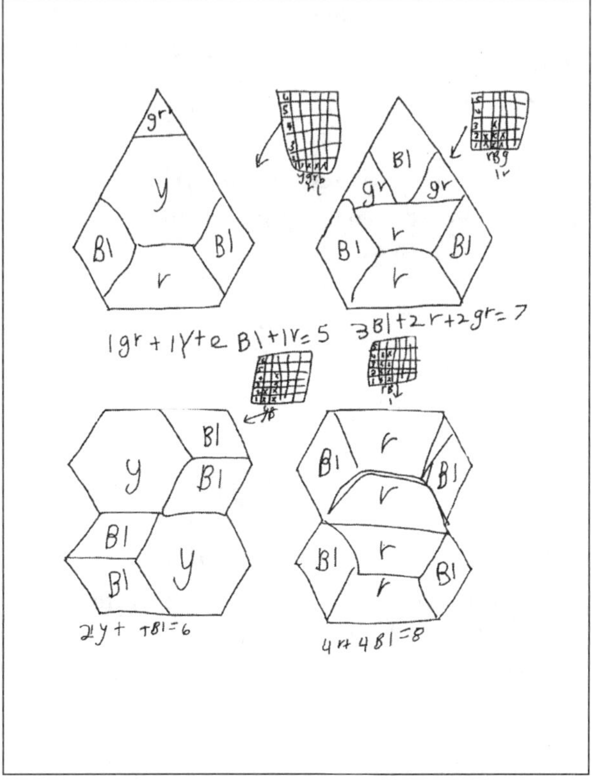

Two More Models to Study: Farmyard and Field Trip

Here are two more Exemplars problems to study, accompanied by student work and annotated rubrics. Note that Farmyard has student work at two levels—not four. Sometimes you will give math tasks for which there are no Novice and Apprentice levels.

If possible, get together with a colleague to discuss these problems. Do you agree with how these were scored? How would you have scored them? Use the student work in the Appendix to practice scoring further. It may take time for you to reach a point in scoring where you feel comfortable using the problems and rubrics as formal assessments—i.e., as assessments that count, and that you share with parents.

Farmyard

Grade Level: K–2

THE TASK

A farmer saw:

4 heads
10 legs
3 tails

What animals did he see? Please show and explain your work, using pictures, numbers, and words.

WHEN TO USE

This performance task should be given after your addition unit is taught and students have had experience with problem-solving activities.

WHAT THIS TASK ACCOMPLISHES

It will show children's mathematical thinking and identify those who have a conceptual understanding of combining numbers in many different ways to equal a given sum. It will offer insights into problem solving in a more general way, and it will allow for creativity.

CONCEPTS ASSESSED AND SKILLS DEVELOPED

- The problem-solving process
- Communication (diagram and/or verbal response)
- Reasoning and decision making
- Recognition and use of patterns
- Number sense
- Addition

WHAT STUDENTS WILL DO

A student will independently solve this problem on the task sheet. If more room is needed, the child may use the back and/or another sheet. The child is encouraged to use diagrams, numbers, and words to indicate mathematical thinking. There are many solutions, and if more than one solution is found, the child is encouraged to show all solutions.

TEACHING TIPS

Introduce the problem by talking about a farm. What kinds of animals live on a farm? Brainstorm a list of farm animals. What do some of the animals look like? Say to students: The farmer in this problem doesn't have a very good view of the animals. All he can see is 4 heads, 10 legs, and 3 tails. Our job is to help him decide what animals he sees.

POSSIBLE SOLUTIONS

This is an open-ended activity that has many possible solutions.

AUTHORS: **Darlene Johnson** and **Sandra Silverman** teach at Oceanview Elementary School in Huntington Beach, California.

EXEMPLARS RUBRIC			
Level	**Understanding**	**Strategies, Reasoning, Procedures**	**Communication**
Novice	• There is no solution, or the solution has no relationship to the task. • Inappropriate concepts or procedures are used.	• No evidence of a strategy or procedure, or uses a strategy that does not help solve the problem. • No evidence of mathematical reasoning. • There were so many errors in mathematical procedure that the problem could not be solved.	• There is no explanation of the solution, t explanation cannot be understood or it i unrelated to the problem. • There is no use or inappropriate use of mathematical representations (e.g., figur diagrams, graphs, tables, etc.) • There is no use, or mostly inappropriate mathematical terminology and notation.
Apprentice	• The solution is not complete, indicating that parts of the problem are not understood.	• Uses a strategy that is partially useful, leading some way toward a solution, but not to a full solution of the problem. • Some evidence of mathematical reasoning. • Could not completely carry out mathematical procedures.	• There is an incomplete explanation; it m clearly presented. • There is some use of appropriate mathem representation. ✓ There is some use of mathematical termi and notation appropriate to the problem
(Practitioner)	✓ The solution shows that the student has a broad understanding of the problem and the major concepts necessary for its solution.	✓ Uses a strategy that leads to a solution of the problem. ✓ Uses effective mathematical reasoning. ✓ Mathematical procedures used appropriately.	✓ There is a clear explanation. ✓ There is appropriate use of accurate mat representation. • There is effective use of mathematical te and notation.
Expert	• The solution shows a deep understanding of the problem, including the ability to identify the appropriate mathematical concepts and the information necessary for its solution.	• Uses a very efficient and sophisticated strategy leading directly to a solution. • Employs refined and complex reasoning. • Applies procedures accurately to correctly solve the problem and verify the results.	• There is a clear, effective explanation de how the problem is solved. All of the ste included so that the reader does not nee how and why decisions were made. • Mathematical representation is actively u means of communicating ideas related t solution of the problem. • There is precise and appropriate use of mathematical terminology and notation.

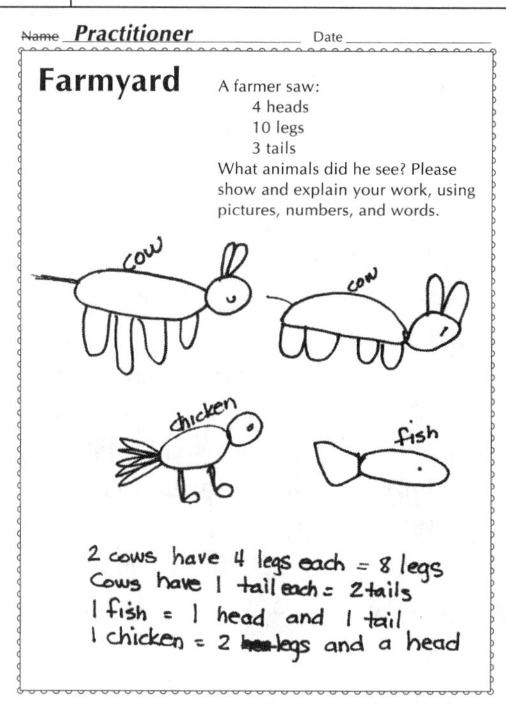
Name *Practitioner* Date

Farmyard

A farmer saw:
4 heads
10 legs
3 tails
What animals did he see? Please show and explain your work, using pictures, numbers, and words.

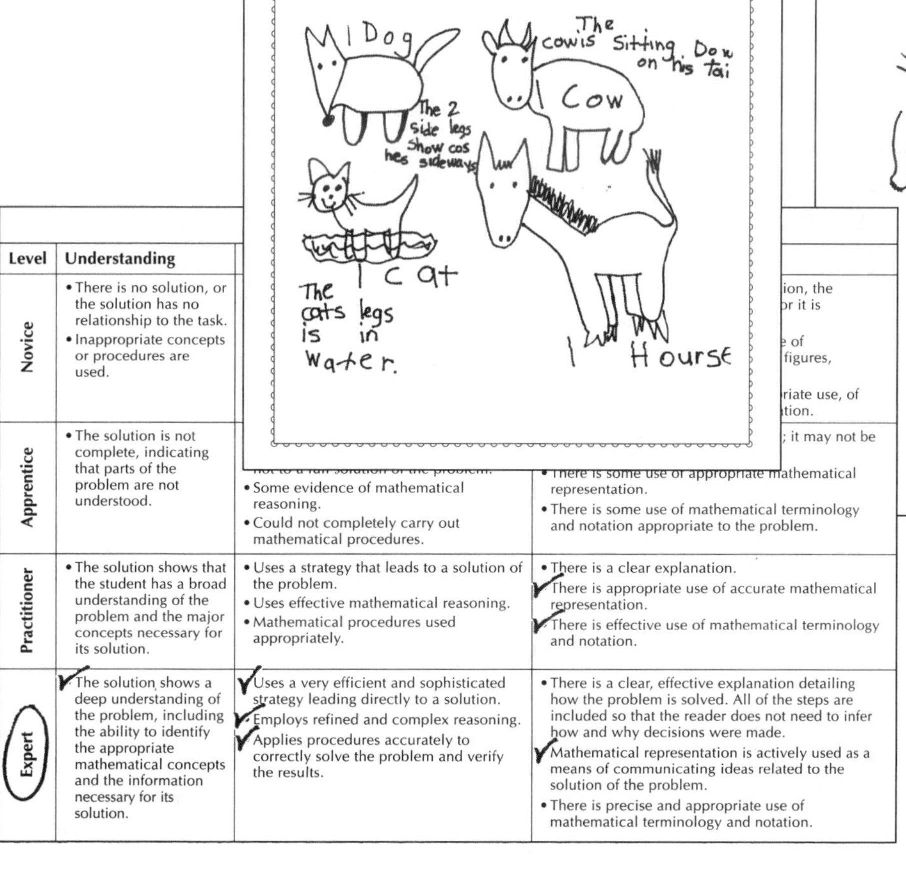
Name *Expert* Date

Farmyard

A farmer saw:
4 heads
10 legs
3 tails
What animals did he see? Please show and explain your work, using pictures, numbers, and words.

Level	Understanding	Strategies, Reasoning, Procedures	Communication
Novice	• There is no solution, or the solution has no relationship to the task. • Inappropriate concepts or procedures are used.		ion, the r it is e of figures, riate use, of tion.
Apprentice	• The solution is not complete, indicating that parts of the problem are not understood.	not to a full solution of the problem. • Some evidence of mathematical reasoning. • Could not completely carry out mathematical procedures.	; it may not be • There is some use of appropriate mathematical representation. • There is some use of mathematical terminology and notation appropriate to the problem.
Practitioner	• The solution shows that the student has a broad understanding of the problem and the major concepts necessary for its solution.	• Uses a strategy that leads to a solution of the problem. • Uses effective mathematical reasoning. • Mathematical procedures used appropriately.	• There is a clear explanation. ✓ There is appropriate use of accurate mathematical representation. ✓ There is effective use of mathematical terminology and notation.
(Expert)	✓ The solution shows a deep understanding of the problem, including the ability to identify the appropriate mathematical concepts and the information necessary for its solution.	✓ Uses a very efficient and sophisticated strategy leading directly to a solution. ✓ Employs refined and complex reasoning. ✓ Applies procedures accurately to correctly solve the problem and verify the results.	• There is a clear, effective explanation detailing how the problem is solved. All of the steps are included so that the reader does not need to infer how and why decisions were made. ✓ Mathematical representation is actively used as a means of communicating ideas related to the solution of the problem. • There is precise and appropriate use of mathematical terminology and notation.

Field Trip

Grade Level: K–2

THE TASK

A class is planning transportation for a field trip.

Cars can take 4 passengers.
Vans can take 6 passengers.
There are 24 students in the class.

How many cars and vans are necessary to take the whole class? Please explain your work, using pictures, numbers, and words. Show as many solutions as you can.

WHEN TO USE

After teaching units on addition and patterns

WHAT THIS TASK ACCOMPLISHES

It will identify students who have a conceptual understanding of combining numbers in many different ways to equal a given sum.

CONCEPTS ASSESSED AND SKILLS DEVELOPED

- The problem-solving process
- Communication (diagram and/or verbal response)
- Reasoning and decision making
- Recognition and use of patterns
- Number sense
- Addition

WHAT STUDENTS WILL DO

Students will independently solve this problem on the attached task sheet. If more room is needed, the child may use the back and/or another sheet. The child is encouraged to use diagrams, numbers, and words to indicate his mathematical thinking. There are several solutions, and if more than one is found, the child is encouraged to show all solutions.

TEACHING TIPS

Set the stage for this activity by talking about going on a field trip, without using a bus. For example: "Today we'll pretend we're going on a field trip. We don't have a bus, but we do have cars and vans. Cars can take 4 passengers, and vans can take 6 passengers. Our job is to decide just how many cars and vans to bring. We're only counting 24 students. We don't count drivers or teachers in the solution."

A Practitioner may be able to clearly identify a correct solution to this task. The Expert will clearly show some organization in his/her solution to be sure nearly all possible combinations of cars and vans are used. In addition, the Expert will use accurate and clear mathematical representation.

POSSIBLE SOLUTIONS

4 vans

6 cars

2 vans and 3 cars

EXEMPLARS RUBRIC			
Level	**Understanding**	**Strategies, Reasoning, Procedures**	**Communication**
Novice (circled)	• There is no solution, or the solution has no relationship to the task. ✓ • Inappropriate concepts or procedures are used.	✓ No evidence of a strategy or procedure, or uses a strategy that does not help solve the problem. • No evidence of mathematical reasoning. • There were so many errors in mathematical procedure that the problem could not be solved.	✓ There is no explanation of the solution, the explanation cannot be understood or it i unrelated to the problem. • There is no use or inappropriate use of mathematical representations (e.g., figur diagrams, graphs, tables, etc.) ✓ There is no use, or mostly inappropriate mathematical terminology and notation.
Apprentice	✓ The solution is not complete, indicating that parts of the problem are not understood.	• Uses a strategy that is partially useful, leading some way toward a solution, but not to a full solution of the problem. ✓ Some evidence of mathematical reasoning. ✓ Could not completely carry out mathematical procedures.	• There is an incomplete explanation; it m clearly presented. ✓ There is some use of appropriate mathem representation. • There is some use of mathematical termi and notation appropriate to the problem
Practitioner	• The solution shows that the student has a broad understanding of the problem and the major concepts necessary for its solution.	• Uses a strategy that leads to a solution of the problem. • Uses effective mathematical reasoning. • Mathematical procedures used appropriately.	• There is a clear explanation. • There is appropriate use of accurate mat representation. • There is effective use of mathematical te and notation.
Expert	• The solution shows a deep understanding of the problem, including the ability to identify the appropriate mathematical concepts and the information necessary for its solution.	• Uses a very efficient and sophisticated strategy leading directly to a solution. • Employs refined and complex reasoning. • Applies procedures accurately to correctly solve the problem and verify the results.	• There is a clear, effective explanation de how the problem is solved. All of the ste included so that the reader does not nee how and why decisions were made. • Mathematical representation is actively means of communicating ideas related t solution of the problem. • There is precise and appropriate use of mathematical terminology and notation.

~~Name~~ *Novice* Date ____________

Field Trip

A class is planning transportation for a field trip.
Cars can take 4 passengers.
Vans can take 6 passengers.
There are 24 students in the class.
How many cars and vans are necessary to take the whole class? Please show and explain your work, using pictures, numbers, and words.
Show as many solutions as you can.

20
+4
+3
+6
33

6Vans 4Cars

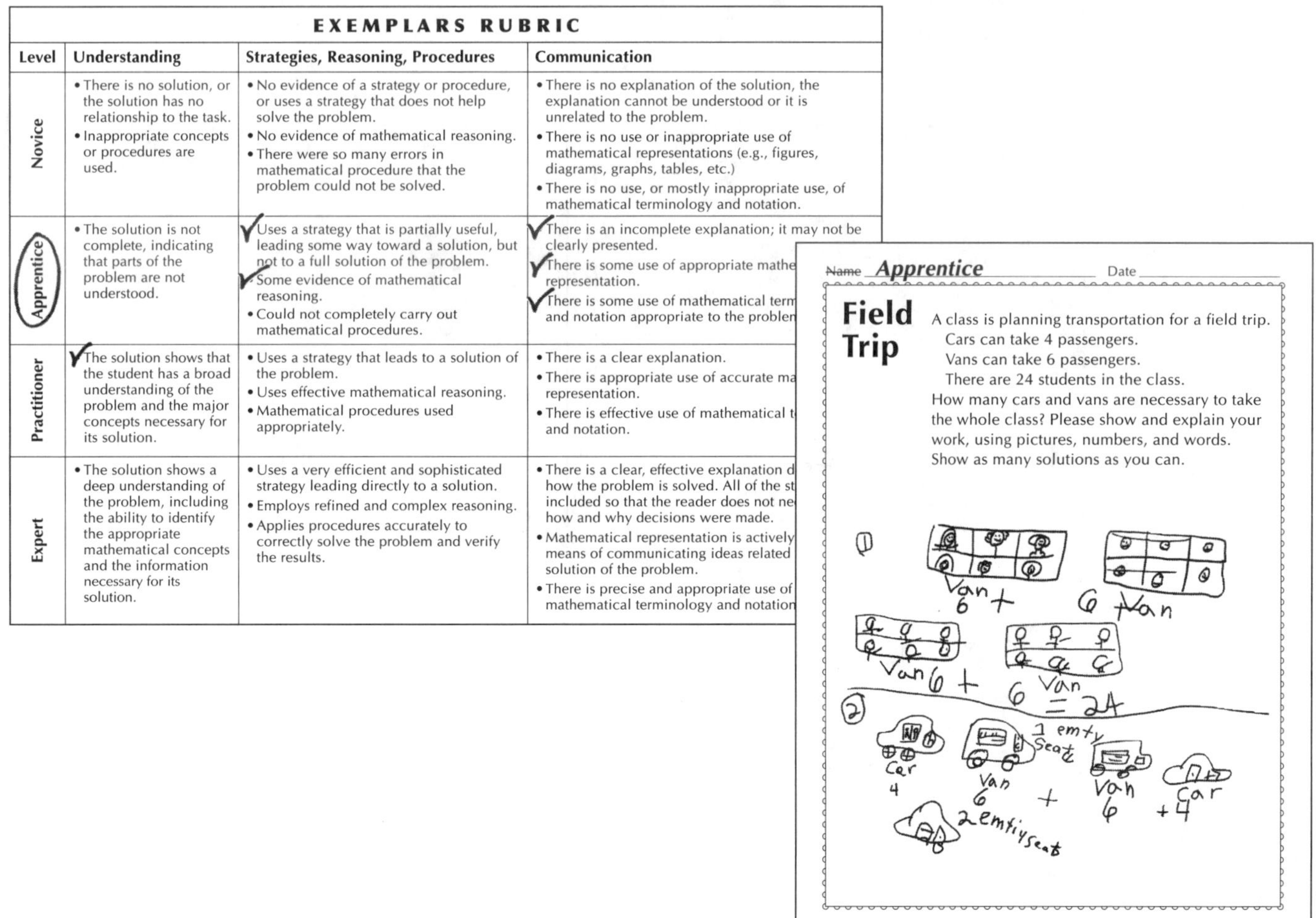

EXEMPLARS RUBRIC			
Level	**Understanding**	**Strategies, Reasoning, Procedures**	**Communication**
Novice	• There is no solution, or the solution has no relationship to the task. • Inappropriate concepts or procedures are used.	• No evidence of a strategy or procedure, or uses a strategy that does not help solve the problem. • No evidence of mathematical reasoning. • There were so many errors in mathematical procedure that the problem could not be solved.	• There is no explanation of the solution, the explanation cannot be understood or it is unrelated to the problem. • There is no use or inappropriate use of mathematical representations (e.g., figures, diagrams, graphs, tables, etc.) • There is no use, or mostly inappropriate use, of mathematical terminology and notation.
Apprentice (circled)	• The solution is not complete, indicating that parts of the problem are not understood.	✓ Uses a strategy that is partially useful, leading some way toward a solution, but not to a full solution of the problem. ✓ Some evidence of mathematical reasoning. • Could not completely carry out mathematical procedures.	✓ There is an incomplete explanation; it may not be clearly presented. ✓ There is some use of appropriate mathe representation. ✓ There is some use of mathematical term and notation appropriate to the problen
Practitioner	✓ The solution shows that the student has a broad understanding of the problem and the major concepts necessary for its solution.	• Uses a strategy that leads to a solution of the problem. • Uses effective mathematical reasoning. • Mathematical procedures used appropriately.	• There is a clear explanation. • There is appropriate use of accurate ma representation. • There is effective use of mathematical t and notation.
Expert	• The solution shows a deep understanding of the problem, including the ability to identify the appropriate mathematical concepts and the information necessary for its solution.	• Uses a very efficient and sophisticated strategy leading directly to a solution. • Employs refined and complex reasoning. • Applies procedures accurately to correctly solve the problem and verify the results.	• There is a clear, effective explanation d how the problem is solved. All of the st included so that the reader does not ne how and why decisions were made. • Mathematical representation is actively means of communicating ideas related solution of the problem. • There is precise and appropriate use of mathematical terminology and notation

~~Name~~ *Apprentice* Date ____________

Field Trip

A class is planning transportation for a field trip.
Cars can take 4 passengers.
Vans can take 6 passengers.
There are 24 students in the class.
How many cars and vans are necessary to take the whole class? Please show and explain your work, using pictures, numbers, and words.
Show as many solutions as you can.

EXEMPLARS RUBRIC			
Level	**Understanding**	**Strategies, Reasoning, Procedures**	**Communication**
Novice	• There is no solution, or the solution has no relationship to the task. • Inappropriate concepts or procedures are used.	• No evidence of a strategy or procedure, or uses a strategy that does not help solve the problem. • No evidence of mathematical reasoning. • There were so many errors in mathematical procedure that the problem could not be solved.	• There is no explanation of the solution, the explanation cannot be understood or it is unrelated to the problem. • There is no use or inappropriate use of mathematical representations (e.g., figures, diagrams, graphs, tables, etc.) • There is no use, or mostly inappropriate use, of mathematical terminology and notation.
Apprentice	• The solution is not complete, indicating that parts of the problem are not understood.	• Uses a strategy that is partially useful, leading some way toward a solution, but not to a full solution of the problem. • Some evidence of mathematical reasoning. • Could not completely carry out mathematical procedures.	✓ There is an incomplete explanation; it may not be clearly presented. • There is some use of appropriate mathematical representation. ✓ There is some use of mathematical terminology and notation appropriate to the problem.
Practitioner	✓ The solution shows that the student has a broad understanding of the problem and the major concepts necessary for its solution.	✓ Uses a strategy that leads to a solution of the problem. ✓ Uses effective mathematical reasoning. ✓ Mathematical procedures used appropriately.	• There is a clear explanation. ✓ There is appropriate use of accurate mathematical representation. • There is effective use of mathematical terminology and notation.
Expert	• The solution shows a deep understanding of the problem, including the ability to identify the appropriate mathematical concepts and the information necessary for its solution.	• Uses a very efficient and sophisticated strategy leading directly to a solution. • Employs refined and complex reasoning. • Applies procedures accurately to correctly solve the problem and verify the results.	• There is a clear, effective explanation detailing how the problem is solved. All of the steps are included so that the reader does not need to infer how and why decisions were made. • Mathematical representation is actively used as a means of communicating ideas related to the solution of the problem. • There is precise and appropriate use of mathematical terminology and notation.

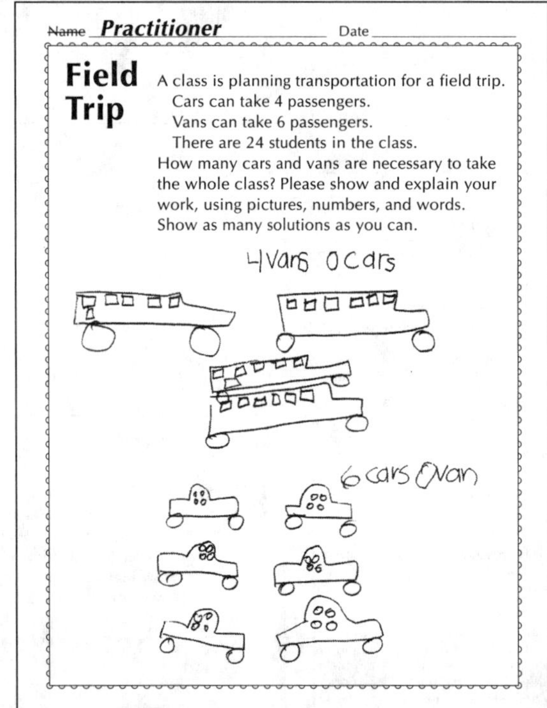

EXEMPLARS RUBRIC			
Level	**Understanding**	**Strategies, Reasoning, Procedures**	**Communication**
Novice	• There is no solution, or the solution has no relationship to the task. • Inappropriate concepts or procedures are used.	• No evidence of a strategy or procedure, or uses a strategy that does not help solve the problem. • No evidence of mathematical reasoning. • There were so many errors in mathematical procedure that the problem could not be solved.	• There is no explanation of the solution, the explanation cannot be understood or it is unrelated to the problem. • There is no use or inappropriate use of mathematical representations (e.g., figures, diagrams, graphs, tables, etc.) • There is no use, or mostly inappropriate use, of mathematical terminology and notation.
Apprentice	• The solution is not complete, indicating that parts of the problem are not understood.	• Uses a strategy that is partially useful, leading some way toward a solution, but not to a full solution of the problem. • Some evidence of mathematical reasoning. • Could not completely carry out mathematical procedures.	• There is an incomplete explanation; it may not be clearly presented. • There is some use of appropriate mathematical representation. • There is some use of mathematical terminology and notation appropriate to the problem.
Practitioner	• The solution shows that the student has a broad understanding of the problem and the major concepts necessary for its solution.	• Uses a strategy that leads to a solution of the problem. • Uses effective mathematical reasoning. • Mathematical procedures used appropriately.	• There is a clear explanation. • There is appropriate use of accurate mat representation. • There is effective use of mathematical te and notation.
Expert	✓ The solution shows a deep understanding of the problem, including the ability to identify the appropriate mathematical concepts and the information necessary for its solution.	✓ Uses a very efficient and sophisticated strategy leading directly to a solution. ✓ Employs refined and complex reasoning. ✓ Applies procedures accurately to correctly solve the problem and verify the results.	✓ There is a clear, effective explanation de how the problem is solved. All of the ste included so that the reader does not nee how and why decisions were made. ✓ Mathematical representation is actively means of communicating ideas related t solution of the problem. ✓ There is precise and appropriate use of mathematical terminology and notation.

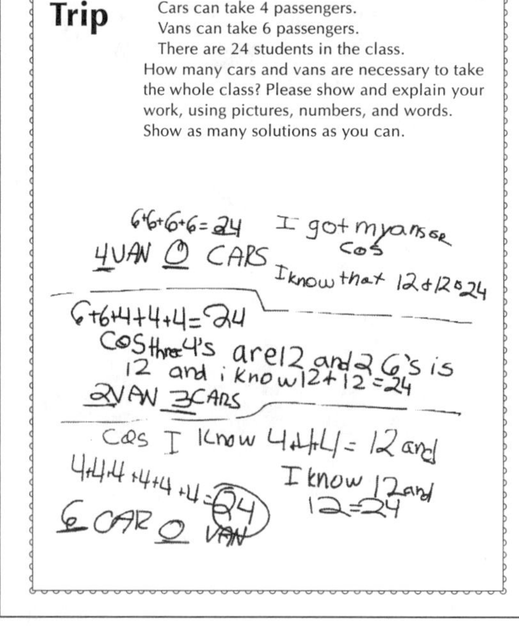

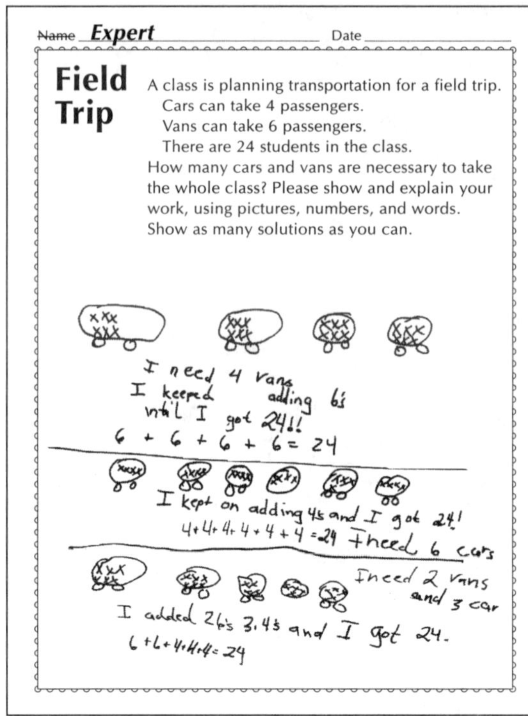

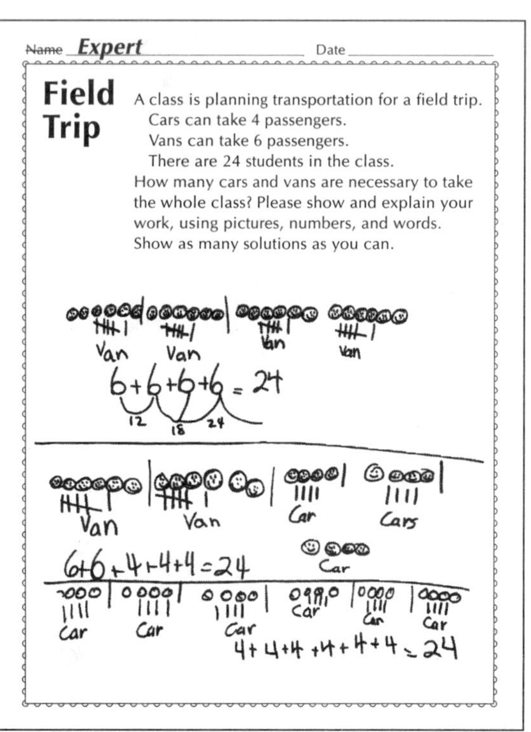

CHAPTER FOUR

Developing Your Own Math Problems

As you develop your own math performance tasks, perhaps the note of caution that appears on a telephoto lens might be useful to keep in mind: "If you are having difficulty focusing, focus on 20 feet and forget about infinity." In other words, don't get overwhelmed by the feeling that you have to overhaul everything you're doing in your math curriculum. Build your assessment problems on the curriculum you have in place right now.

Planning Assessments: Key Questions to Ask Yourself

As you plan for any assessment, it's helpful to ask yourself the following questions:

- What is it that I want my students to know and be able to do this year?
- Given the expectations that I have for teaching math in this school year, what do I want to focus on for this particular assessment?
- Will the assessment provide an opportunity for students to demonstrate their ability to use the skills they have learned?

Interweave Math Problems Into the Curriculum

Susan Nellen, a first-grade teacher at the Marion Cross School in Norwich, Vermont, wants to assess her students' understanding of combinations of numbers. Here, she shares the reasons why she uses Flags to accomplish this goal.

Flags

Grade Level: K-2

THE TASK

Using three colors—red, blue, and white—in a vertical stripe pattern, how many different flags can you make? Each flag must use all three colors but must be different from the others.

WHEN TO USE

After teaching a unit on patterns and combinations

CONCEPTS ASSESSED AND SKILLS DEVELOPED

- Problem solving
- Reasoning
- Communicating
- Patterning
- Combinations

WHAT STUDENTS WILL DO

Some students use the guess-and-check strategy. They draw a flag and check to see if they used that combination before. Other students guess-and-check and then see patterns that help to make other combinations. A few students organize their approach by color—they find all the combinations starting with white, then blue, then red.

Let's look at what Susan took into consideration before she presented Flags to her class.

THE CONTEXT

In social studies, we were studying different cultures and countries and their flags.
In math, we were classifying and sorting different attributes of flags. We had also been doing a good deal of work with two- and three-color patterns.

TIME REQUIRED FOR THE TASK

About a half hour

SETUP AND MATERIALS

I used the French flag as the model for the problem. Make a sheet with two rows of 4 blank flags in the same design as the French flag. Hand out sheets and red, white, and blue crayons to students.

POSSIBLE SOLUTIONS

red, white, blue
red, blue, white
white, red, blue
white, blue, red
blue, red, white
blue, white, red

Author: **Susan Nellen** is a first-grade teacher at the Marion Cross School in Norwich, Vermont.

Steps Susan Takes

Before presenting the problem to students, Susan makes sure it will help assess students' knowledge of patterns *and* their ability to apply that knowledge to an unfamiliar math challenge. She also identifies how the problem reflects the NCTM Standards. She writes these notes:

Know: Students will demonstrate their understanding of patterns as a way to organize their mathematical thinking.

Do: Students will be able to name attributes, sort according to attribute, and create patterns by varying the combinations of attributes. They will also demonstrate their ability to use the guess-and-check strategy for problem solving.

Tie to NCTM Standards: The Flags problem directly relates to the standards regarding problem solving, reasoning, communication, patterning, and combinations.

3 Key Planning Questions

Susan has brought together critical planning questions before using an assessment task.

1. She identifies what it is she wants her students to know and be able to do.
2. She identifies a specific problem-solving task that might help her to assess the students' computation skills as well as their capacity to solve complex, real-world problems.
3. She reviews the NCTM Standards and makes certain that her problem is meeting them.

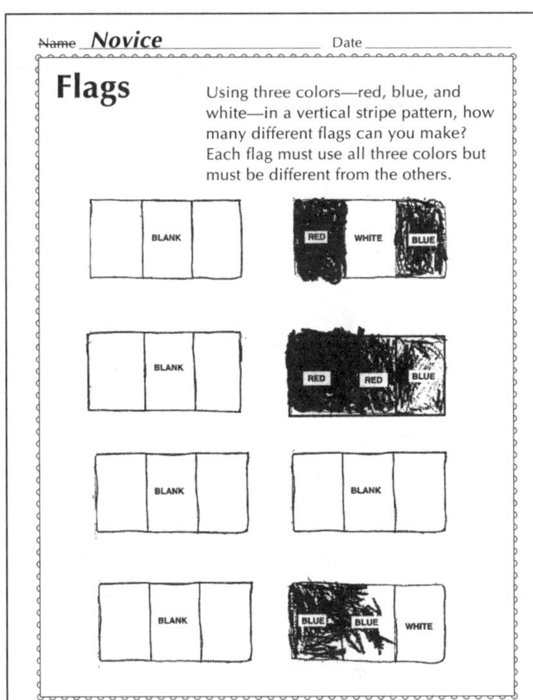
Name Novice Date

Flags

Using three colors—red, blue, and white—in a vertical stripe pattern, how many different flags can you make? Each flag must use all three colors but must be different from the others.

Inappropriate concepts are applied (two colors on the same flag). No evidence of a strategy or procedure. When asked, the student has no explanation for the drawing. The student does not appear to understand the problem.

The solution is not complete, and the student is using a strategy that is only partially useful. There is some evidence of reasoning because the student seems to start with a pattern (e.g., red, then blue, then white), but that breaks down and, in fact, the student rejects a flag that should be a part of the collection.

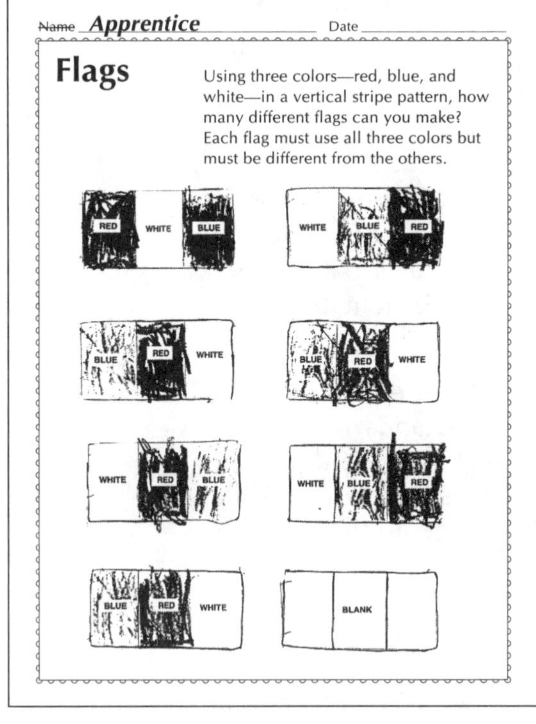
Name Apprentice Date

Flags

Using three colors—red, blue, and white—in a vertical stripe pattern, how many different flags can you make? Each flag must use all three colors but must be different from the others.

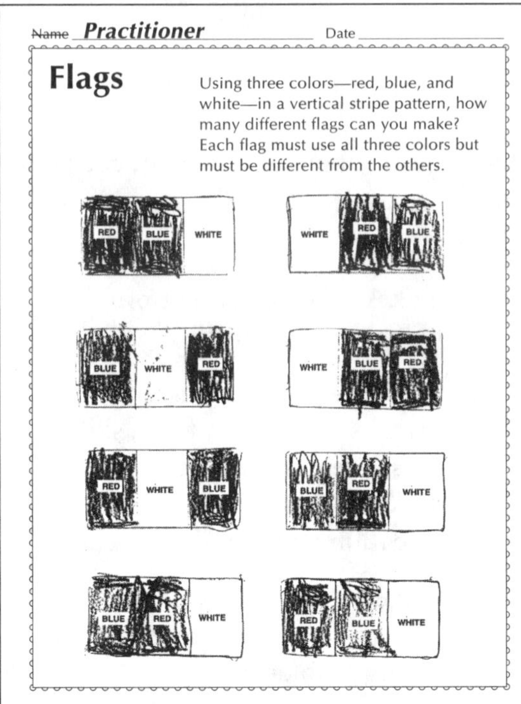
Name Practitioner Date

Flags

Using three colors—red, blue, and white—in a vertical stripe pattern, how many different flags can you make? Each flag must use all three colors but must be different from the others.

This student finds all six flags. The two flags at the bottom that are crossed out indicate she checked to see if there were any duplicates. When asked if she thought she had found all the flags, the student uses the rejected flags as a reason she was fairly confident that all the flags were found.

This student not only finds all the flags but also goes about it systematically, first finding all the ways starting with red, then blue, then white. The student is confident that all the flags are found using this strategy.

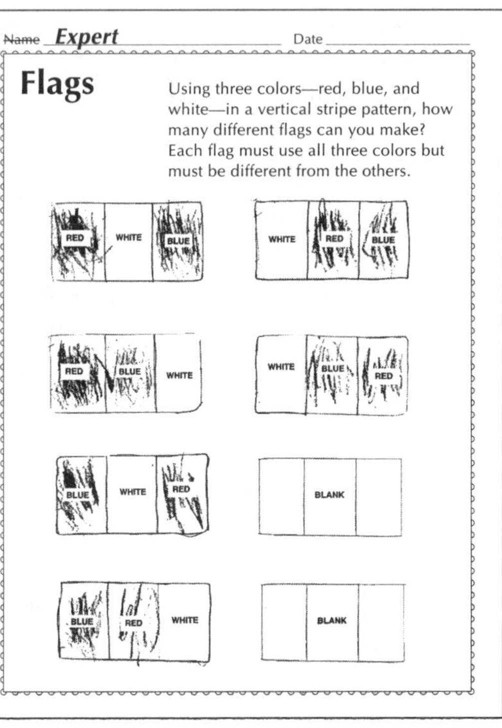
Name Expert Date

Flags

Using three colors—red, blue, and white—in a vertical stripe pattern, how many different flags can you make? Each flag must use all three colors but must be different from the others.

AN ASSESSMENT-PLANNING WORK SHEET	
What are the topics and concepts that I cover during the school year?	
What are the skills that I expect my students to develop over the school year?	
What do I expect my students to do so that they are behaving as mathematicians?	
When I read the NCTM Standards, how do I translate those standards back into the grade that I teach?	

Your Turn: A Planning Work Sheet

Use a planning work sheet (see example above) as a guide to help you identify what it is you want students to know and be able to do over the course of the year.

Many teachers find it useful to plan on the basis of the customary cycles of the school year that jibe with report card periods and/or conferences. In addition, you may want to list the thematic units that you have planned within each of these cycles. Ask yourself: How can I connect mathematics to the cross-curricular themes I plan to cover this year?

On page 41 is another planning sheet for you to map out your assessments.

Once you have worked out a plan for what you want students to know and be able to do, you are ready to tackle the next question: How will I know if they are getting there?

When thinking about assessment, consider the following questions from first-grade teacher Kathy Ernst:

- What makes this assessment problem engaging for my students?
- What are the aspects of learning I want to assess, e.g., math facts, skills, concepts, strategies, cooperative learning skills, dispositions, communication skills, and so on?
- What range of competencies might the students reveal to me through their work on this problem?
- What questions can I pose to reveal my students' thinking and understanding?
- How will my students and/or I document their work?
- What opportunities exist for the students to assess their own learning?

Name ____________________ Date ____________________

ASSESSMENT OF STUDENT THINKING: A Planning Grid

	Problem Solving	Reasoning	Communication	Statistics and Probability	Geometry and Spatial Sense	Fractions
Standardized achievement subtests						
Matrix sampling						
NAEP/state tests						
Teacher-made criterion-referenced tests						
Teacher observation						
Journals/writing samples						
Checklists						
Interviews						
Exhibitions						
Inventories						
Portfolios of student work						
Child study anecdotal records						
Extended projects						
Critical incidents						
Other						
Columns across top of grid						
Problem solving						
Reasoning						
Communication						
Statistics and probability						
Geometry and spatial sense						
Fractions						

Components of a Good Problem-Solving Task

As you develop your own assessment problems, you'll have moments when you wonder if a problem is rich enough, and whether it really gives students opportunity to demonstrate their problem-solving skills. When in doubt, here are some ideas to keep in mind:

- Problem solving is the process of confronting a novel situation, formulating connections between given facts, identifying the goal, and exploring the possible strategies for reaching the goal.
- Develop your own working definition of an exemplary problem. For example, a quality problem...

  Δ is meaningful and engaging to students; its context motivates students to want or need to find a solution.

  Δ contains no immediate or obvious way to determine a solution. The solution is not obtained only by recall of facts and operations.

  Δ may be solved through using different strategies and may yield multiple solutions.

  Δ can be extended mathematically or integrated with other curriculum areas.

  Δ is at an appropriate skill level.

In Line: Is It an Effective Assessment?

Let's look at the problem In Line, which Cindy Pierce, a first-grade teacher at Marion Cross Elementary in Norwich, Vermont, designed.

Does it meet the criteria for a quality problem established above?

In Line

Grade Level: K–2

THE TASK

Five students are going on a treasure hunt. They need to line up with a girl as the line leader and a boy as the line follower. There are three girls and two boys. Show how many different ways they could line up and still follow the rules. Write a key so that we know what code you have used to show girls and boys. Your code may have shapes, colors, numbers, letters/words, symbols, or diagrams.

WHEN TO USE

After students have had experience organizing information

WHAT THIS TASK ACCOMPLISHES

It provides several solutions. Students need to create a key and use it appropriately. They need to organize possibilities using trial and error or by recognizing the solutions and how they are organized.

CONCEPTS ASSESSED AND SKILLS DEVELOPED

- Problem solving
- Organization
- Making and using a key
- Reasoning

THE CONTEXT

"Lining up is a big event in my classroom. Students are always problem solving ways to line up on their own. While doing the problem, we discussed possible ways to code girls and boys. Several students suggested using pink for girls and blue for boys. Others suggested long hair for girls and short hair for boys. Another suggested dresses for girls and pants for boys. When we were going over the solutions, we discussed sexism and stereotypes for about thirty minutes. To explain sexism, we compared it to racism, which led to a huge discussion of Martin Luther King, Jr."

TIME REQUIRED FOR THE TASK

15–20 minutes

TEACHING TIPS

Clarify that one code should be used for all of the solutions found. Have children generate a list of code possibilities.

SUGGESTED MATERIALS

Some students may wish to use manipulatives to try their possibilities before they write them.

POSSIBLE SOLUTIONS

g=girl and b=boy

gbggb

gggbb

ggbgb

Look back at the guidelines for a quality problem-solving task. How well does In Line meet the guidelines?

Is it meaningful and engaging to students?

Yes, In Line presents students with a problem that affects their everyday lives. It is something that is important to them. Cindy's students became so engaged in the problem that their conversation moved to a discussion of stereotypes, sexism, racism, and fairness.

Is there an immediate or obvious way to determine a solution? Or is it challenging?

For children this age, the problem is a challenge. They need to think carefully, and then discuss with one another how they might begin. It requires them to develop an organizational scheme such as a key or chart.

Can it be solved through multiple strategies and yield multiple solutions?

Yes, In Line has three solutions, and there are many ways to solve the problem. Some of Cindy's students used manipulatives while others worked with crayons or pencil and paper. Many students used trial and error as a strategy.

Can it be extended mathematically or integrated into other curriculum areas?

Yes, students extended their thinking to issues of fairness within their classroom and beyond it as a result of thinking about this problem. The Expert benchmark in this problem also pursued additional solutions to confirm that there were only three.

Is it appropriate in skill level?

Yes; since In Line allowed for multiple strategies and entry points, almost all of Cindy's students were able to find at least one solution.

Seizing those Math Moments

One day, Cindy's students bickered over seating arrangements for lunch. Cindy made the most of the moment, recognizing the opportunity for her students to solve a math problem and a social problem in one fell swoop. She recalls:

"We had been using pattern blocks for some of our computation activities and had had discussions about the similarities and differences among the shapes. The tables in our classroom are different shapes (trapezoid, hexagon, circle, and rectangle). Every lunch, students get into arguments about how many people are allowed to sit at each table. Some were under the impression that all tables could have only four students even though we have two larger tables with six sides or spots.

"Tired of having to play referee every lunchtime, I pulled out the pattern blocks, and we talked about the shapes and number of sides. We looked at the tables and counted the number of sides. We practiced counting and keeping track of the sides by numbering them. We practiced counting the sides when the shapes were put together in ways that created extra sides. The children soaked up the concept because they were invested in it; sorting out the dos and don'ts of lunchtime seating really mattered to them."

Cindy then presented the problem on page 45 to her class.

Name *Novice* Date

In Line Five students are going on a treasure hunt. They need to line up with a girl as the line leader and a boy as the line follower. There are three girls and two boys. Show how many different ways they could line up and still follow the rules. Write a key so that we know what code you have used to show girls and boys. Your code may have shapes, colors, numbers, letters/words, symbols, or diagrams.

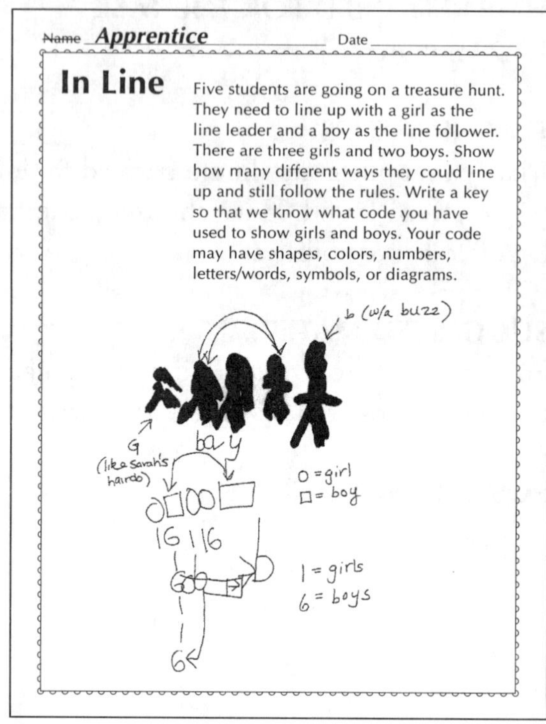

Name *Apprentice* Date

In Line Five students are going on a treasure hunt. They need to line up with a girl as the line leader and a boy as the line follower. There are three girls and two boys. Show how many different ways they could line up and still follow the rules. Write a key so that we know what code you have used to show girls and boys. Your code may have shapes, colors, numbers, letters/words, symbols, or diagrams.

Use this problem after you have done a unit on geometry or shapes with your students.

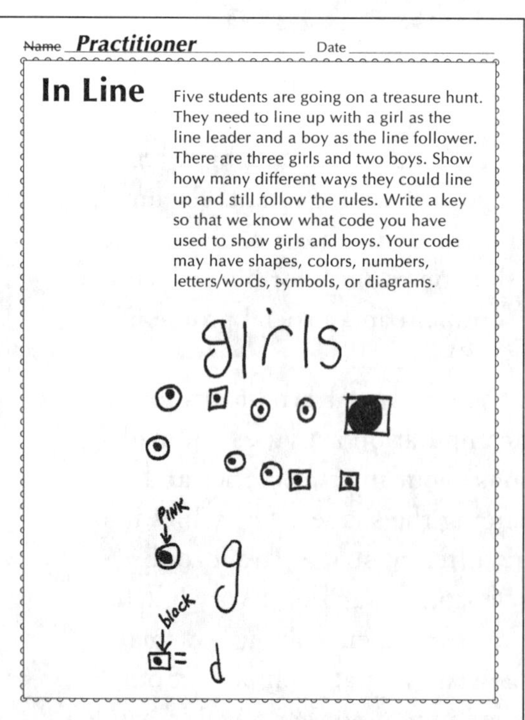

Name *Practitioner* Date

In Line Five students are going on a treasure hunt. They need to line up with a girl as the line leader and a boy as the line follower. There are three girls and two boys. Show how many different ways they could line up and still follow the rules. Write a key so that we know what code you have used to show girls and boys. Your code may have shapes, colors, numbers, letters/words, symbols, or diagrams.

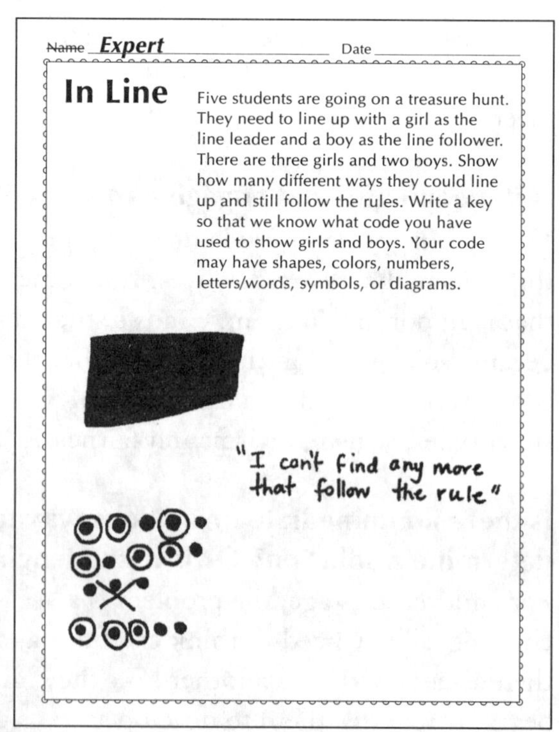

Name *Expert* Date

In Line Five students are going on a treasure hunt. They need to line up with a girl as the line leader and a boy as the line follower. There are three girls and two boys. Show how many different ways they could line up and still follow the rules. Write a key so that we know what code you have used to show girls and boys. Your code may have shapes, colors, numbers, letters/words, symbols, or diagrams.

Pentomino

Grade Level: K–2

THE TASK

Use the three pentominoes that are provided to make as many different shapes with twelve sides or less. Use the following three shapes:

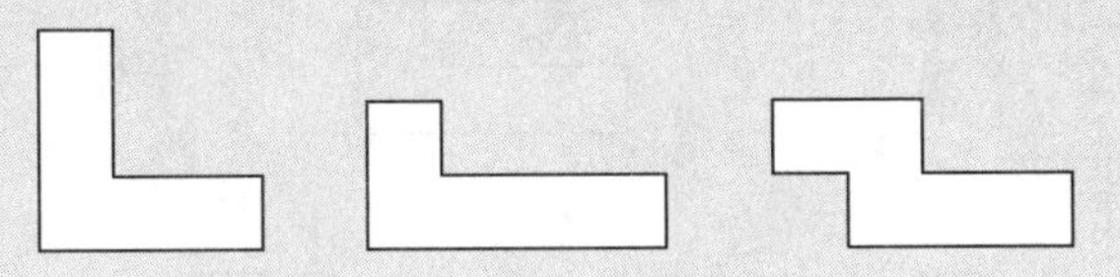

WHEN TO USE

After teaching a unit on estimation, shapes, and geometry

WHAT THIS TASK ACCOMPLISHES

Counting sides of geometric shapes

Turning, flipping, and sliding pieces to make shapes

Tracing

CONCEPTS ASSESSED AND SKILLS DEVELOPED

- Estimation
- Geometry and spatial problem solving
- Problem solving
- Communication
- Reasoning
- Connections

WHAT STUDENTS WILL DO

Make hollow shapes or pictures with the pieces

Use the same shapes several ways in the same solution

Make a shape with the pentominoes, count the sides, and trace the pieces if the shape fits the rule

Make a shape, trace the pieces, and count afterward

Make a shape, and trace just the outside so that the solution isn't clear

Include the number of sides on each pentomino, even when they aren't on the outside of the shape

Use only two of the pentominoes

When recording the sides, skip sides or count a side twice if two pieces meet on that side

Make shapes without the individual shapes traced and without numbers

Erase one of the pieces, and move it to a place that creates fewer sides

Put the pieces corner to corner, creating extra sides

TIME REQUIRED FOR THE TASK

20–30 minutes

TEACHING TIPS

Sort the pentomino sets ahead of time so that each student has the three pentominoes.

For the second half of first grade and for second grade, have the students find the three pentominoes.

Have kids play with a few pattern blocks to make shapes with as many or as few sides as they can.

Find shapes around the room with a given number of sides.

Identify the number of sides in shapes around the room.

Remind students to show solutions with tracing each pentomino.

With older or more advanced kids, have them try making shapes with the maximum number of sides being between 8–10.

SUGGESTED MATERIALS

- A set of pentominoes for each student so

that she/he can have the same three pentominoes

- Pencils

Author: **Cindy Pierce** is a first-grade teacher at the Marion Cross School in Norwich, Vermont.

POSSIBLE SOLUTIONS

These are some solutions that a teacher came up with:

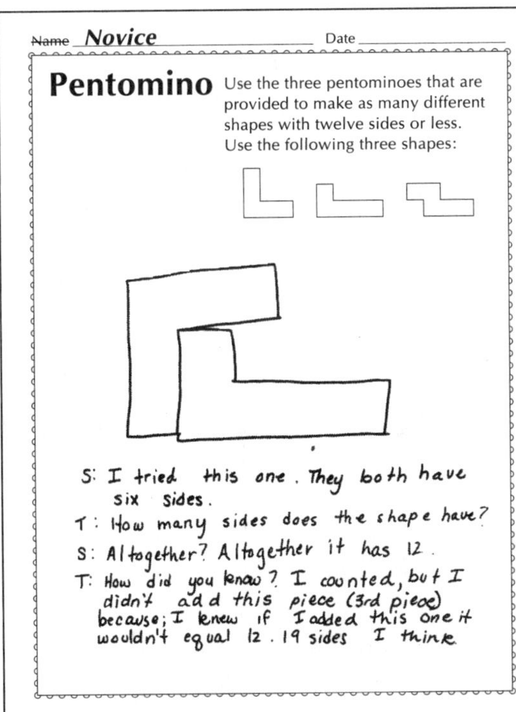

Name Novice Date

Pentomino Use the three pentominoes that are provided to make as many different shapes with twelve sides or less. Use the following three shapes:

S: I tried this one. They both have six sides.

T: How many sides does the shape have?

S: Altogether? Altogether it has 12.

T: How did you know? I counted, but I didn't add this piece (3rd piece) because; I knew if I added this one it wouldn't equal 12. 19 sides I think.

This student was unable to find a solution. He only used two of the pieces. Each of the L-shaped pentominoes has six sides; he put the two shapes together and considered the eight-sided shape to be a twelve-sided shape (six add six). There were so many errors in the procedure that the problem could not be solved. He thought he couldn't add the third piece because it would add six more sides, which would break the rule of twelve sides or fewer. The explanation is unrelated to the problem, because the student didn't understand the direction to put three shapes together to make one shape.

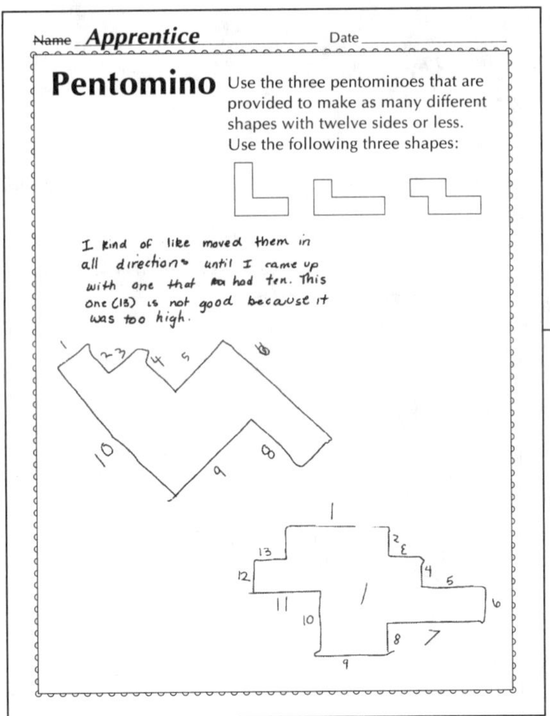

Name Apprentice Date

Pentomino Use the three pentominoes that are provided to make as many different shapes with twelve sides or less. Use the following three shapes:

I kind of like moved them in all directions until I came up with one that had ten. This one (18) is not good because it was too high.

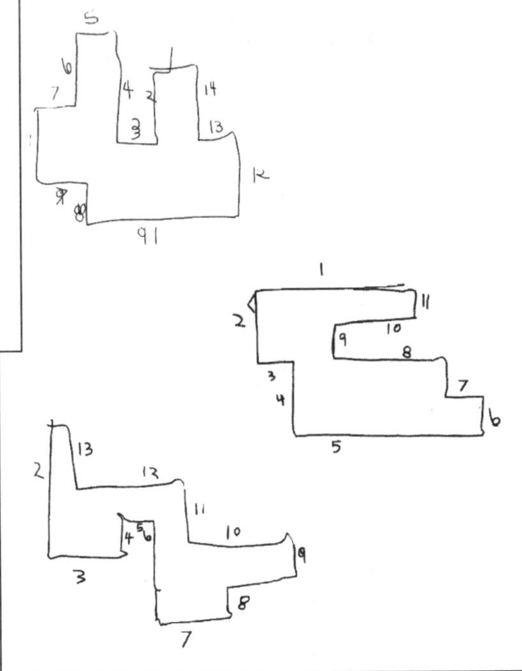

This student used a strategy that is partially useful, leading to one solution. The problem was not clearly presented; she didn't trace each pentomino so that it is not clear how the shapes were arranged to make the shape. This student counted sides after she traced so that she ended up with only one solution that fit the rule and two that had over twelve sides. The ability to recognize that one of her solutions didn't fit the rule shows evidence of mathematical reasoning.

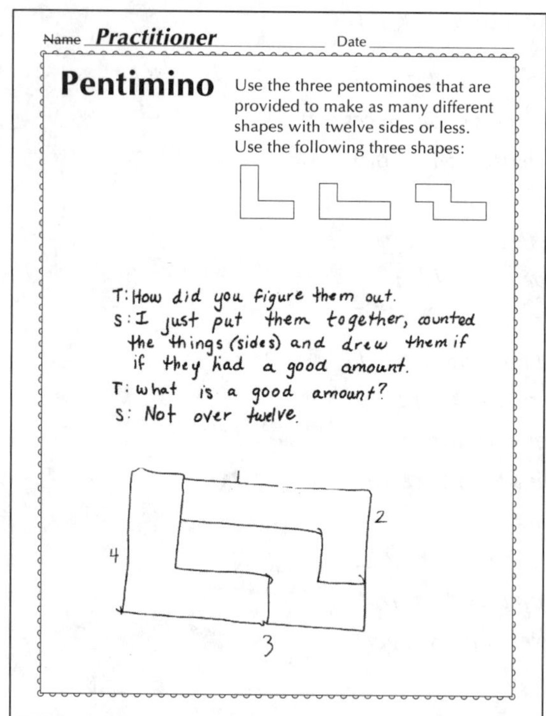
Name *Practitioner* Date

Pentimino Use the three pentominoes that are provided to make as many different shapes with twelve sides or less. Use the following three shapes:

T: How did you figure them out.
S: I just put them together, counted the things (sides) and drew them if if they had a good amount.
T: what is a good amount?
S: Not over twelve.

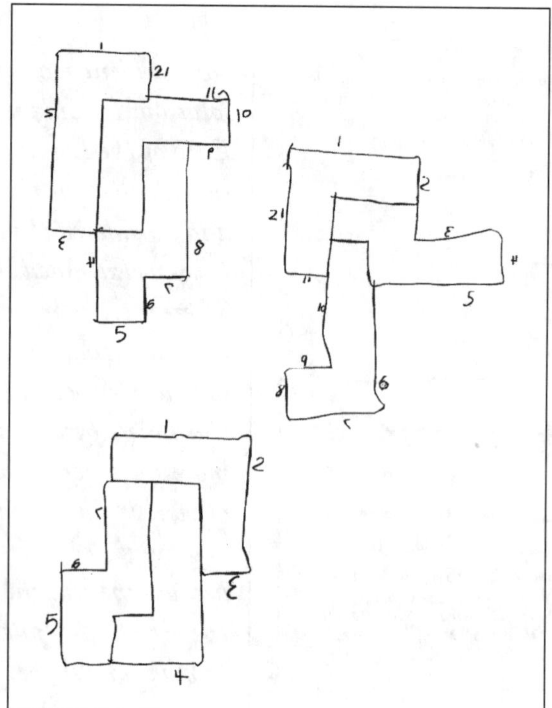

This student used a strategy that led to four solutions. He has a broad understanding of the problem, finding solutions with 4, 8, and 12 sides. Three out of four were traced clearly, and the number of sides was recorded accurately. This student communicated his solution clearly but used unspecific terms such as "things" (sides) and "good amount" (12 or fewer).

This student has a deep understanding of the problem and was confident that she had five correct solutions. She used an efficient strategy that led directly to a solution, and counted the sides of the shapes before tracing. She ended up with five correct solutions that are clearly presented with each piece traced and sides recorded. This procedure enabled the student to find multiple solutions and verify the results. The explanation includes all the steps so that the reader does not need to infer how and why decisions were made.

Name *Expert* Date

Pentomino Use the three pentominoes that are provided to make as many different shapes with twelve sides or less. Use the following three shapes:

S: I have 5 solutions
T: How did you figure it out?
S: I tried all different ones. The ones that fit the rule, I put the #'s down of how much there was. I counted first then traced.

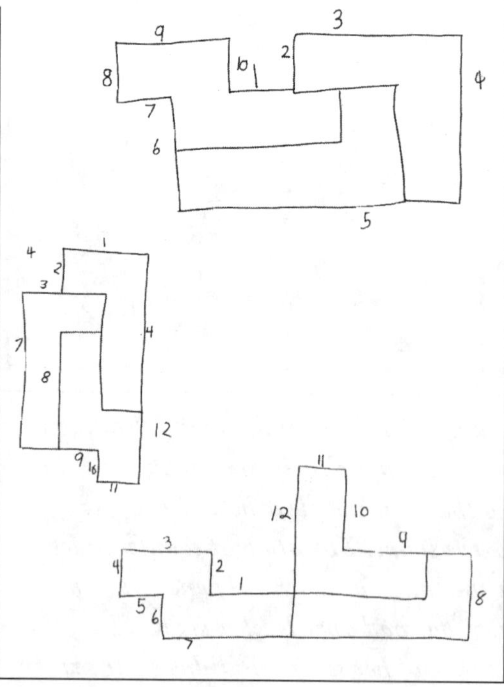

The Common Thread: All Three Problems Are Relevant to Children's Lives

As you can see from Flags, In Line, and Pentomino, the problems your students work with can originate from your math curriculum, a social problem in the classroom, a question about bus routes, a good picture book, a story told in sharing circle—the sky's the limit. While you keep your eyes and ears out for engaging problems, keep this thought in mind: Your goal is to assess your students' ability to apply mathematics in *different* situations. Look for moments outside of math time to see if they can put their knowledge into action. For example, if your students are learning about bar graphs in math and you hear them one day debating which kind of cola tastes better, invite them to take a class-wide cola preference poll. Ask them: How are you going to collect your information? How will you show your results? Leave the rest to them. Chances are, students will use bar graphs to show the results of the poll (and if they don't, then you have a clear picture of what you need to reteach).

CHAPTER FIVE

Creating a Comfortable Environment for Assessment

Now we'd like to describe the climate of trust that needs to be built in the classroom if, in fact, students will be comfortable enough to give their best problem-solving performance. We need to create a classroom community in which both teacher and students know how to give and receive feedback. What we say to our students—and what we encourage them to say to one another—must:

- be constructively stated
- be specific and easily understood
- provide a suggested path for improvement
- be within the range of the learner's capabilities at that time

Give specific praise: Positive comments about work such as "well done" and "great" are important but insufficient by themselves. The student needs to know specifically which part of the work was well done. Give feedback along the lines of: "Jon, I like the way you were able to draw this picture to help you understand the problem," or "Susan, you did a great job. You were able to show me the steps you took to solve the problem" or "I see that you were having difficulty understanding the problem. I wonder if it might have been helpful to try to organize what you know with a chart like this."

Show what you expect: Remember that constructive and specific feedback needs to be modeled constantly—not just during math class—if you expect students to learn how to give feedback to one another.

Model effective feedback with math circles: Once you have done a sufficient amount of public commentary, you can start a math circle. Here's how it works: Have all students sit in a circle, bringing their math work papers to the circle. Invite a student to describe how she interpreted the problem, what her solution was, and what strategies she used to arrive at a solution. Then start a conversation about the student's work, guided by questions such as: What did you notice about Lisa's problem solving? Do you agree with her solution? If not, where do you see a difference between her solution and yours?

How do you explain the difference? Does anyone have another way of seeing this problem?"

12 Questions that Encourage Reasoning

Gradually you will be able to have rich discussions about problem solving in the classroom. As your questioning techniques move from questions requiring right or wrong or yes or no answers to more open-ended, thought-provoking ones, you will find that the climate for giving and receiving feedback will develop. The NCTM has provided us with a set of questions that empower learners to answer through mathematical reasoning. Here are some:

1. Why do you think that?
2. How did you reach that conclusion?
3. Does anyone have the same answer but a different way to explain it?
4. Can you convince the rest of us that that makes sense?
5. Is that true for all cases?
6. How could you prove that?
7. Do you see a pattern?
8. Can you predict the next one? What about the last one?
9. What is alike and what is different about your method of solution and hers?
10. What ideas that we have learned before were useful in solving this problem?
11. Have we ever solved a problem like this one before?
12. What uses of mathematics did you find in the newspaper last night?

Try presenting one of these questions to your students every day. You can write a question on the board so that students can ask them in their problem-solving groups or in the math circle. In time, your students will internalize the thinking that these questions evoke. They will start to ask—and answer—the questions themselves, without prompts.

Grouping that Engages all Students

Many of us struggle with how to group students effectively, especially during an assessment. As we move away from homogeneous grouping, we are left with the unsettling question of how to make certain that all students remain interested, challenged, and supported. Here are some ways of grouping that have proven successful:

Use the Exemplars rubric (see page 125). The rubric will help you organize your thinking about grouping. Consider groups that mix Novices, Apprentices, Practitioners, and Experts. This will provide the group with a range of math knowledge for problem solving. A good time to use this grouping pattern is when you believe that students, through their work together, can raise their level of performance. Remember that as few as two students can be a group, though you should avoid pairing students who may have a peer tutoring relationship during an assessment. Remember, the assessment needs to show you how your students are thinking mathematically. For that reason, you want the student to work in as self-directed a way as possible.

Randomly select students to work together for short-term projects. In fact, you can even use this kind of grouping to give children practice in recognizing attributes and patterns. Invite students to create a group by lining up according to size; they then count off for grouping. Or children can form groups on the basis of those who are wearing shoes that tie, those who are wearing velcro closings, those who have shoes that buckle; all people with brown eyes, or all people with blue eyes, all people with glasses; or all people who walk to school and those who ride the bus. In other words, group according to attributes. Let the students make up the next way to group.

Group by interest. Students are often motivated by particular areas of interest, such as dinosaurs, skateboarding, and bugs. When you put those students together, they often perform beyond your expectations. They may be more willing to persevere with problem solving.

Enlist students' ideas. Invite students to help you develop a list of grouping ideas to use throughout the year (a good exercise for combinations and permutations). You might say to kids: "We are going to work in groups many times this year. Your task is to help me design many varied and unusual ways that we can form groups. Once you have brainstormed as many different ways as possible to group, design a scheme that ensures that everyone in the class has the opportunity to work with everyone else at least once. No one works with anyone more than two times. We need to have a rotation for groups that will work over five days." Developing many different grouping practices helps students understand that all members of the classroom can work with one another.

Taking the time to build these values and routines in the classroom will pay off. The classroom will be perceived as a safe place for taking the necessary risks for learning, as well as for performing optimally during assessment time.

Grouping for Assessment Time

Once students are accustomed to many different grouping patterns, they will easily work in cooperative groups during assessment time. You will need to decide whether you want the students to work individually or in groups. Many teachers vary the practice so that they acquire information about the children in different contexts. Keep in mind the following ideas:

- You do not have to give all students the same problem. You can make choices about which problems will be most appropriate for different students. The concept is to make certain that you are raising the floor for some students without lowering the ceiling for others!
- While students are working in groups, observe interactions and make anecdotal records regarding student thinking and participation.
- After students perform the assessment, share what you observed about the group process with students.
- Working on math tasks with peers provides good practice for a higher-stakes game, such as the state or national performance-based tests. The sharing of knowledge helps students build a bigger repertoire of strategic approaches to problems; group work can "loosen up" children's thinking. That said, make certain that you provide opportunities for individual performance practice, since this mirrors the format of the state and national tests.

Thoughtful Room Arrangements

The way you arrange the furniture in the classroom can support problem-solving behaviors. Here are some tips from teachers we've worked with:

Think about traffic flow. On graph paper, construct a map of your room to scale. Work out where you would like to have your bookcases, your worktable or conference space, your desk. Make certain that you have created a good traffic pattern for the students to move about the room. The people who design supermarkets know that the way the aisles are arranged and the products are organized on the shelves determines consumer behavior. We can use the same thinking for our classrooms. Think about how you can control the patterns of traffic in the classroom, and carefully plan what goes on the shelves and walls the students pass on their way from one location to another. For example, one teacher and her students decided to arrange the desks in groups of four. She placed the learning centers around the edges of the room. Bookshelves were used as low dividers so that students were sufficiently separated from one another for group work. She had a special meeting place where students were able to work as a whole group.

Use groups of four to foster independent and group work. Arrange the desks in groups of four so that students can work easily with one another. This also provides the option for individual work. If the class is not divisible by four, have a group of two or three.

Turn the room arrangement into a math challenge. A wonderful way to start the school year is to have the students develop a scheme for grouping arrangements. This will start the year with an exciting math problem using combinations and permutations. How many different ways can we arrange the desks into groups so that we never have a group size larger than four? If you set the pattern early that desks can be arranged and rearranged, you will find it easier to regroup and rearrange as you learn more about the strengths and behaviors of the students.

Making Children Comfortable During Assessment

When you give a paper-and-pencil test to students, do you coach them as they perform? It is unlikely. Yet when we give students performance tasks that require more thinking, figuring things out, and working with others, there's a temptation to get involved! When you use the assessments in this book or design ones of your own, remember that they are an opportunity to see what your students do when you are not *reminding* them about what to do!

Here are tips to help you define your role during an assessment (your students should have a clear idea about your role ahead of time):

Before giving the assessment, set up a sheet like this (see next page) to help you document your students' conversations. During the assessment, keep the sheets on a clipboard, and note what you observe. If you feel uncertain about a specific student, you can ask questions in a conference with the child or set up an informal task to test his understanding.

These are a few of the behaviors you might want to look for, listen for, and note; you probably have others to add.

Names of students in this group: ____________________ ____________________
Assessment focuses for this task:
Degree of each student's involvement: (expect that if you question any member of the group, they will be able to tell you how they are approaching)
Evidence of different ways of thinking and presenting knowledge:
Examples of risk taking: (you want to hear comments like "Maybe we should try it another way")
Evidence of willingness to stick with the problem even though it may be difficult:

More Tips for Managing Assessment Time

Remember, students respond favorably to consistent patterns. When assessment is taking place in the classroom, here are some structures that work particularly well:

- Provide a clear set of written instructions.
- Be certain to delineate how you will be scoring the problem-solving task—give students the scoring rubric (*see Appendix for reproducible rubrics*).
- If you are using groups, designate roles and responsibilities for group members.
- Let your students know that you are wearing your assessment hat. Many classroom teachers we've worked with have been amazed by student performance when teachers refrain from answering questions such as "Is this what you want?" or "What am I supposed to do next?"
- If it is obvious that the task is too difficult for a student, don't coach the child through the problem. Instead, document what you have learned about the student's thinking, and allow the student to perform successfully by

immediately giving him an easier but similar kind of problem.

Commonly Asked Questions About Assessment

Here are questions that frequently come up when we talk with teachers about Exemplars assessment problems:

Should I use the Exemplars problems in nonassessment situations?

Yes, as we discussed in Chapter 2, you can use the problems in all phases of teaching math. Teachers Amy Morse and Carol Amico use Exemplars problems for these purposes:

Exploration: Before you begin a unit, you can learn how well-prepared your students are as a class by giving them a problem that uses the skills you will be teaching. See how they approach it.

Diagnosis: You can also gain a good deal of insight into individual students by giving them problems, either before you begin or while you are teaching a particular set of skills. This will help you focus on the needs of particular students.

Instruction: Problems also serve as a wonderful vehicle for teaching. Working together as a whole class or in groups, as students brainstorm and develop strategies, construct mathematics representations, and look for meaning and extensions, they will be actively teaching one another important problem-solving and other mathematics skills.

Assessment: Assessment will give you a sense of how your class and individual students are applying mathematics skills in different situations.

How often you give students formal assessments will depend on your needs and your school's assessment approach. For example, the district in which Terry Ferrarone works (Katonah-Lewisboro) gives assessments four times a year. They share the Performance Task Rubric with parents, along with benchmark papers, so parents get a crystal-clear picture of their children's work and progress.

How often do I use the problems with my students?

Some teachers like to do a problem of the week, each week. Others, particularly those who are just beginning to use authentic assessment in mathematics, feel more comfortable doing a problem every other week.

How can I continue to make mathematical problem solving important without taking a lot more time from my curriculum?

Some teachers work to integrate problem solving into their curriculum by making interdisciplinary links. For example, if they are studying the theme of community, they might ask students to estimate the distance each child in the classroom travels to go from home to school. They might then find ways to check their estimates. Finally, they might compare the distance that they travel to school with the distance the teachers and administrators travel. Do all people who work in our school live in our community? Perhaps do a bar graph of how many people who work in our schools live in our community and how many do not. Using authentic assessment problems such as this one, teachers can see if their students can choose the appropriate operations (fractions or division, for example) to solve the problem.

Try to use the authentic problems as a way to compact your curriculum rather than seeing it as an "add on." Perhaps three or four well-designed problems may serve as a substitute for some of your traditional unit in fractions, for example. Perhaps you can find a way to do less practice sheets for addition and subtraction because you have substituted some more authentic and richer problems that require student application of those skills. Since you always have to be concerned with time management, you will have to think about how authentic tasks can replace some of your existing work.

Should students be working in groups on these problems, or should they work independently?

When people work in the world outside of the classroom, they sometimes have the option of working alone or working in groups. Some people find that their work is best served by group interaction. Others find that they need time to think alone before working with others. You probably have a microcosm of those work styles in your classroom. Some students will need "think time" before working with a group, while others may need "talk time" in order to think! For that reason, you may want to provide working options for students.

The most important aspect of using these math problems as assessment is that you have individual as well as group information about performance.

We recommend that students be given the opportunity for working on problems in groups. You can move around the classroom, clipboard in hand, and "note" information about group process and thinking. We also recommend that students be responsible for individually writing up the answer to and their reasoning about the problem. We have found, over time, that students cannot write about what they do not understand. If they have merely been hitchhiking on another student's reasoning, they will be unable to do the individual write-up. That said, there are times when the student knows more than he/she is able to communicate through writing. If this is the case, you may want to interview the child.

Remember, the assessment of individual performance guides your instructional decisions. The assessment of group performance guides your decisions about how to group for the best gain in social construction of knowledge.

How do I differentiate my role as teacher/coach from my role as assessor?

This is one of the most difficult tasks for teachers. You care about your students. You want them all to be successful. You worry about a student's self-esteem if he or she cannot solve a problem. As a result, you try to help your students along. You give hints, direct students to try certain strategies, remind them of work they have already done. But the end product is really a demonstration of both teacher and student.

The questions posed by the problems in this book are:

- What does the student do when he or she is uncertain about what to do?
- What strategies does the student apply?
- How much does the student apply from previous knowledge?
- Does the student choose an appropriate mathematical operation for this particular problem? In other words, how does the student work in the absence of teacher as coach?

Here are suggestions to help you maintain distance from teaching while assessing:

- Announce to your students that today is an assessment day and that you will be observing how they go about solving problems without asking you for help. This does not preclude their receiving help from one another. Use the "three-before-me" strategy ("You must ask at least three other students in the class before you ask me").

- Carry a clipboard for noting your observations. You can discuss what you will be observing with the students in advance. For example, "Today I will be looking for how well you listen to one another as you try to solve the problem. These are the indicators of good listening I will focus on...."

- Don't make eye contact with students or engage in distracting conversations. Often students will try to draw you into the group. They see you nearby and, if they catch your eye, ask, "Is this right?" "Is this what you want us to do?" By avoiding eye contact (get busy note-taking), you may avoid getting drawn into the group's work.

- Provide feedback about your observations after the problem-solving session is over. Tell them what you observed, especially noting positive and constructive work and behavior. This will serve two purposes: (1) students can learn from the feedback; and (2) students will know you are serious about your role as assessor.

CHAPTER SIX

Using Problem-Solving Math Portfolios

We have presented many ways of working on math problem solving. We now need to think about how we can collect student work over time that will serve as evidence of growth for the student, parents, and others. Whereas more traditional tests might provide significant information about a student's computational skills, the portfolio can provide significant information about a student's ability to meet the standards set for problem solving, reasoning, and communication.

What is a portfolio?

Portfolios contain a carefully selected body of work that represents evidence of growth toward defined learning goals. To understand the potential of portfolios as a means of collecting and assessing student work, let us begin with a story.

Judy graduates from high school and is applying for her first job. She has a large folder of material that she has saved from her work in high school. She rents a loft in New York City and buys her first piece of furniture—a drafting table. She starts to draw various designs and waits anxiously by the phone for a response to her résumé from two advertising agencies. She has been working diligently for two days and is surrounded by sheets of paper with various drawings and designs. Finally, the phone rings. One advertising agency wants Judy to come in for an interview. She hangs up the phone and looks at the work all over the floor as well as from her high-school folder.

Judy examines each piece and says, "I think I will take this piece because it shows my creative use of color. And this one shows how I use design images and words in an original format. These pieces will fit with other pieces I have done over the last year and will show how I have grown over time." She takes each of the pieces and carefully places them in her portfolio.

Judy arrives at her interview, and the person from the agency asks her to show her portfolio and explain why she chose the work that she did. As he listens to her explanations, he engages in a conversation about her work. Together they talk about the standards of the company, Judy's concept of her "personal best," and whether there is a fit between the external standards of the company and Judy's self-assessment about her work. Perhaps the potential employer asks her to go home and construct some pieces to the agency's specifications. Perhaps the person gives her valuable feedback about her work. Perhaps the person and Judy decide collaboratively about whether her work will satisfy the next set of interviewers in the agency.

Below is a list that may help to remind you about this story and what it exemplifies about portfolios:

Collection. Judy had a folder containing her present work as well as that from her last three years in high school. If she did not have this folder, she would not have sufficient work to draw from that would demonstrate her performance and progress over time.

Selection. When Judy knew that she was going for an interview and that her work was to be judged, she selected key pieces from her collection. She studied the employer's standards. She tried to make selections that would be representative of her best work.

Reflection. The only way that the interviewer could understand the work was if Judy was able to describe why she chose each piece. The reflection helped the interviewer know what was in the artist's mind as the basis for presenting a particular piece. Judy was able to show evidence of her performance over time; she could demonstrate her commitment to learning.

Direction. Whether Judy gets the job or not, she will have a better sense of where she wants to go with her work. She will also have the opportunity to reflect on her work in light of the conversation with the interviewer and the standards held by the employer. That conversation will help her reevaluate her goals and help her set a further direction for her work.

Much like Judy's portfolio, your students' math portfolios can contain selected pieces of work produced over time, chosen according to a set of criteria, with reflections on each piece and on the portfolio as a whole.

Define a Purpose and an Audience

You need to decide why you are developing portfolios. Is it for next year's teacher? For the student? For the parents? For the administration? For the purpose of improving self-evaluation?

Portfolios need to have an audience—they need to be read and responded to by someone. We have focused the question of audience on parents, students, this year's teacher, next year's teacher. These different audiences may need different pieces in the portfolio. Let's review the function of each audience in looking at the portfolio:

Tips for Sharing Portfolios With Parents

When parents review their child's portfolio, they need to be able to see how their child is doing over time. As you know, parents' number-one concern is: How is my child progressing in relation to standards that have been set for this developmental level? To answer this, show parents benchmark papers for tasks—then show them their child's work. This sets the scene for parents and helps them evaluate their children's work with more insight and impartiality.

Many parents want to know how they can support their child so that he will work to improve performance. Although the focus is often on direction (what are the goals for the child?), be certain to help the parents celebrate the growth and strength in their child's work.

Our experience suggests that parents often do not know how to read their child's work for its strengths. Here are some tips:

- Suggest to parents that they remain positive when discussing their child's work. Suggest that they preface their remarks with supportive phrases like "I see that you have used...." This kind of language encourages rather than discourages kids. Most important, remind parents to notice what is *there* rather than looking for what is missing.
- Ask students to write a note to their parents telling them what to look for and reflecting on what they consider to be important about the pieces of work in the portfolio. This helps parents know what to look for.
- Invite students to attend the conference and lead the discussion about their portfolio.
- Invite the students to talk about the direction they feel their work should take.
- Ask the parents, if their child is not at the conference, to write a letter to her, describing what they saw as the strengths of her work.
- Provide a place where parents can read the portfolio while they are waiting for their turn to conference.
- If you have student-led conferences, allow for students to stay in the room and continue discussing their work with their parents while another student's conference begins. Some teachers define four discrete areas in the room and have four simultaneous conferences going on at once. This allows for a longer conference time for parents without extending the conference time in which the teacher is available.
- Role-play conferences with the students, and prepare them for the conferences by helping them pull their portfolios together and think about what they want to tell their parents about their work.
- If there is no significant care giver who can come for the conference, make certain that another teacher, counselor, or administrator conferences with the child about his portfolio.

The Portfolio: Benefits for Students

Since we will not be able to follow students throughout their lives, helping them to develop the capacity for self-evaluation may be our most important contribution to their lifelong learning. During the process of portfolio selection and reflection, students are engaged with self-evaluation (*see Student Reflection Form on next page*). They are required to think about their work and to look for indicators of good problem solving. The portfolio becomes a showcase for the strengths in a student's performance. (Though, at times, you may want to have students compile a portfolio that shows a range of work, demonstrating the variety of things they have encountered, which may include work that is not their best.)

A portfolio marks time, progress, growth, and change. The reflection serves as an opportunity for the student to become self-analytical and self-examining. Since the quality of the work is ultimately in the hands of the student, this process brings the student face-to-face with what they produce.

The Portfolio: Benefits for You

The portfolio can provide additional data necessary for making critical judgments for report cards and conferences with parents. It

Name ______________________ Date ______________

Student Reflection Form

Why I chose this math problem for my portfolio: ______________________

What I learned about myself as a mathematician from doing this math problem: ______________________

How I think I can improve as a mathematician: ______________________

also serves as a magnifying lens, bringing into high definition the way the student sees himself as a problem solver. For example, sometimes the student will choose a particular problem to include in the portfolio that will surprise you. You may not have considered that piece of work as a good example of how the student meets quality standards. However, when you talk with the student about the selection, you may find that the student chose the work because he felt that it was an example of how he was taking risks in problem solving. The conversation about what is valued by the student in relation to what has been stressed as valuable by you is an important one.

It is difficult to watch a flower grow! The portfolio shows progress over time—information about growth that is often so slow that it is imperceptible. Celebration of small changes becomes a part of building a student's confidence in her capacity to do the work of problem solving. Celebrating a student's progress also builds a relationship of trust between you and the student, the benefits of which will ripple in all sorts of wonderful ways.

Portfolios: Benefits for Next Year's Teacher

When students enter the classroom in September, they are often suffering from summer amnesia! They behave as if there never was a last year in school. Many teachers use the previous year's portfolios to remind each student of where he/she was before summer vacation. They invite children to reexamine their work, set goals for this year, and share their work with a partner who may not have come from the same classroom. At this time, teachers establish their expectations for the students. The portfolio serves as an entry opportunity for building the learning community.

Often when a teacher notices learning difficulty, the portfolio will provide insight that will be helpful for instructional decisions. In addition, resource teachers find the portfolio one of the most useful sources of data to inform their work with the student.

Categories of Work for the Portfolio

You need to think about the categories of work you would like students to include in their portfolios. We have already discussed the possibility of one category being problem solving. Are there other categories of work that would be of significance, such as examples of application of math problem solving at home?

In addition, you need to think about range of work. We have already shown you how to score student work on a continuum from Novice to Expert. It will be especially useful to have examples of that range of work within a student's portfolio so that you can see development over time.

The kinds of artifacts that you might put in the portfolio would include, based on the work we have been describing in this book, (1) examples of student work in problem solving; (2) the student's reflection regarding that work; and (3) a range of work from Novice to Expert, with student reflection on his understanding of growth over time.

Choosing the Work

One of the main purposes of the portfolio is to develop children's capacity for self-reflection and self-assessment. With that in mind, the student should choose the examples for the portfolio. The choice of work should be related to the specific categories and with specific criteria in mind. Occasionally you may feel as if the work chosen is not the student's best example. In that case, you may choose work, as well. However, you should then confer with the student and ask why the student chose the piece that she did. You can shift the conversation to explain why you chose particular pieces instead. This conversation can be very valuable because it illuminates for students the basis for your judgment.

Defining the Terms

We need to establish criteria for evaluating the work within the portfolio. If, for example, we are looking at a student's drawings, what is it we are looking for? How can we allow the drawing to speak to us and not narrow its meaning for the child or for ourselves as assessors?

Examining children's work in the portfolio helps us ask the question: Why is this work here? What do we look for to inform us about the student's progress? How can we develop an explicit language for looking at children's work that helps us as teachers better interpret what we mean by the Standards?

If the portfolio is to be useful to students, you must provide instructional time for learning how to be more analytic in choosing pieces for the portfolio. In one elementary school, teachers follow these procedures to teach students about selection and reflection:

1 Read a piece of work carefully with the whole class. Show the work on an overhead so that the students can follow along with you. Analyze the work according to the criteria.

2 Break the class into pairs, and have them study one piece of work they have selected to put into the portfolio.

3 Invite students to have a conversation about what they see in the work. Caution them not to judge the work with subjective words such as "neat" or "great work." The students need to use language that describes understanding the problem, reasoning, strategies, and communication of results.

4 After the pairs have completed the task, ask them to each write their reflections. The conversation with peers helps to provide students with a comfortable language for their reflection.

Other Math Assessment Ideas

Introduce students to the concept of keeping a math journal. In journals and logs, children reflect about math problem solving, which enhances their communication skills.

Encourage personalization of math folders. Allow students to decorate them. Also make certain that students can have easy access to folders that they can be managed by the students and not by the teachers. Include a record-keeping sheet so that students can record the results of their performances.

Write a letter to parents. Explain the role of problem solving in your math curriculum; explain the thinking behind the NCTM Standards and why involving kids with complex problems instead of just computational skills is key to the kind of mathematical thinking needed in the present as well as future. Be certain to show where you will be assessing computational skills and how they are important to problem solving. This will help you gain parental support for the students' work as well as your own.

Share with students your assessment criteria. This is important so that they learn to measure their own performance and develop the ability to self-evaluate. Make sure that students keep track of their accuracy and precision along with their problem-solving strengths.

Schedule student conferences. Help your students to become better at self-evaluation by confering with them when you are writing report cards. Many teachers have found it very powerful to have the students at the parent conference so that they can talk about their work with their parents and teacher present. This is a good place to set goals with students for future work.

Going Beyond "Wadja Get?"

Creating an instructional climate and language for assessment and feedback is critical to the ultimate success of our students. We need to bring assessment beyond "Wadja get?" to include "Howdja get it?" The correct answer to a problem is still very important in authentic assessment; valuing "howdja get it"—the process—is not meant to undermine the solution. Our goal is to describe student learning in a way that expresses the student's real capabilities. We must enlarge and enhance our students' demonstrations of learning. In the world of school, nothing elevates a student's self-esteem more than knowing that he is a capable learner. You cannot feel good about yourself in school unless you can perform in the academic realm. We can use assessment and feedback as a source for building a student's self-esteem by talking about the real work of thinking and problem solving. When we only talk about scores, we reduce the importance of the learner to a number.

In the Appendix that follows, there are 20 Exemplars problems that you can use to get started with your students. These are just a sampling of the problems that have come from Exemplars' national network of teacher contributors. You can have access to many more problems—along with teaching tips, solutions, rubrics, and benchmark papers—at the kindergarten through second-grade level, as well as grades three to five and six to eight, by contacting:

Exemplars
271 Poker Hill Road
Underhill, VT 05489
(800) 450-4050
E-mail: exemplar@sover.net
Web page: www.exemplars.com

Or you can order a CD-ROM complete with 180 math tasks, benchmark student work, scoring procedures, tools for planning and grading, as well as staff development material for teachers. Please write, call, or e-mail:

Technology Pathways
12 Crooked Mile Road
Westport, CT 06880
(203) 457-9089
E-mail: Hunsickerc@aol.com

Appendix

Name ______________________________ Date ____________________

Muffins

Muffins cost 25¢. How many ways can you pay for the muffin? Please show and explain your work using pictures, numbers, and words.

Muffins

Teaching Tips Page

Grade Level: K–2

THE TASK

Muffins cost 25 cents each. How many ways can you pay for the muffin? Please show and explain your work, using pictures, numbers, and words.

WHEN TO USE

Give this performance task *after* you teach a unit on money.

WHAT THIS TASK ACCOMPLISHES

It will identify students who have a conceptual understanding of coin recognition, value, and exchange properties.

CONCEPTS ASSESSED AND SKILLS DEVELOPED

- The problem-solving process
- Communication (diagram and/or verbal responses)
- Coin recognition
- Coin value
- Money counting
- Money exchange

WHAT STUDENTS WILL DO

Students will independently solve this problem on the task sheet given to them. If more room is needed, they may use the back and/or another sheet. Students may trace coins, if desired. They are encouraged to use diagrams, numbers, and words to indicate their mathematical thinking. There are many solutions to the problem. If children find more than one solution, they should show all they discover.

TEACHING TIPS

Ask yourself: What do the kids need to know (e.g., equivalencies of money, how to add and subtract)? Have I taught these skills?

Set the stage for this activity by talking about going to the store to buy a muffin. For example, "Today we'll pretend we're going to the store. We want to buy a muffin. Muffins cost 25 cents each. We have a lot of coins in our pockets and have to decide which coin or coins we want to use to pay for the muffin." Avoid modeling the problem or altering the task sheet.

POSSIBLE SOLUTIONS

1 quarter

2 dimes, 1 nickel

2 dimes, 5 pennies

1 dime, 2 nickels, 5 pennies

1 dime, 1 nickel, 10 pennies

1 dime, 15 pennies

5 nickels

4 nickels, 5 pennies

3 nickels, 10 pennies

2 nickels, 15 pennies

1 nickel, 20 pennies

25 pennies

Name ______________________________ Date ____________________

Kite Shop

Spring is a time to look for a kite to catch the wind. Look at the kite shapes, and use your pattern blocks to fill them. You need to find different solutions for each kite. Write a math sentence, and make a chart or graph for each kite you fill in.

Kite Shop

Teaching Tips Page

Grade Level: K-2

THE TASK
Spring is a time to look for a kite to catch the wind. Look at the kite shapes, and use your pattern blocks to fill them. You need to find different solutions for each kite. Write a math sentence, and make a chart or graph for each kite you fill in.

WHEN TO USE

After teaching about pattern blocks and geometric shapes. Tie in to a springtime exploration of kite flying.

WHAT THIS TASK ACCOMPLISHES

It provides an opportunity for students to find more than one solution, to practice using their spatial sense, and to practice creating math sentences and representations.

CONCEPTS ASSESSED AND SKILLS DEVELOPED

- **Geometry and spatial sense:** modeling, drawing, and describing geometric ideas
- **Statistics and probability:** collecting, organizing, and describing data; interpreting displays of data
- **Whole number computation:** selecting and using computational techniques appropriate to the specific problem
- **Problem solving:** using problem-solving approaches to investigate and understand mathematical content; relating problems to everyday situations
- **Communication:** relating physical materials to mathematical concepts; reflecting on and clarifying thinking about mathematical situations
- **Reasoning:** justifying answers and solution processes; drawing logical conclusions about mathematical situations
- **Connections:** applying mathematical thinking to solve problems in other disciplines, such as science, social studies, and art

WHAT STUDENTS WILL DO

Students will utilize their visual and spatial skills to fill in the different kite shapes in more than one way. The students will use pattern blocks to explore different solutions and then choose two for each shape to record. They will provide a math sentence for each solution and then chart or graph their designs in a logical format.

TIME REQUIRED FOR THE TASK

60 minutes

TEACHING TIPS

Put the following 3 kite shapes on a sheet for each student, drawing them so that pattern blocks fit inside them.

Read Gail Gibbon's beautifully illustrated *Catch the Wind!* to spark discussions about kite designs. Discuss the correct names for the different pattern blocks and their attributes.

Prior to doing the problem, students will need a variety of opportunities to practice using their visual and spatial skills, using pattern blocks, pentominoes, and tangrams. Students will also need many opportunities to write math sentences and use graphing skills.

SUGGESTED MATERIALS

- Literature that illustrates a variety of kite shapes
- Pattern blocks for small groups

- Sheet with 3 different kite shapes to fill in with pattern blocks for each student
- Pencils, colored pencils, or crayons
- Graph paper (optional)

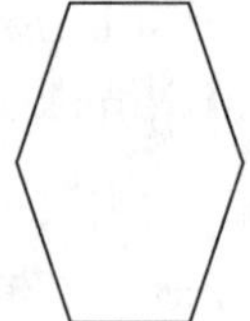

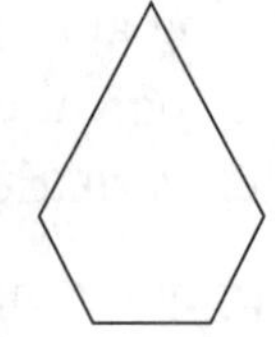

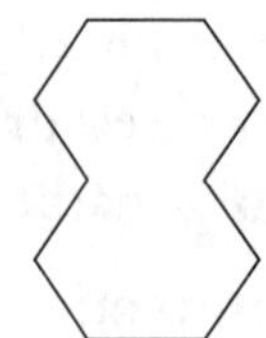

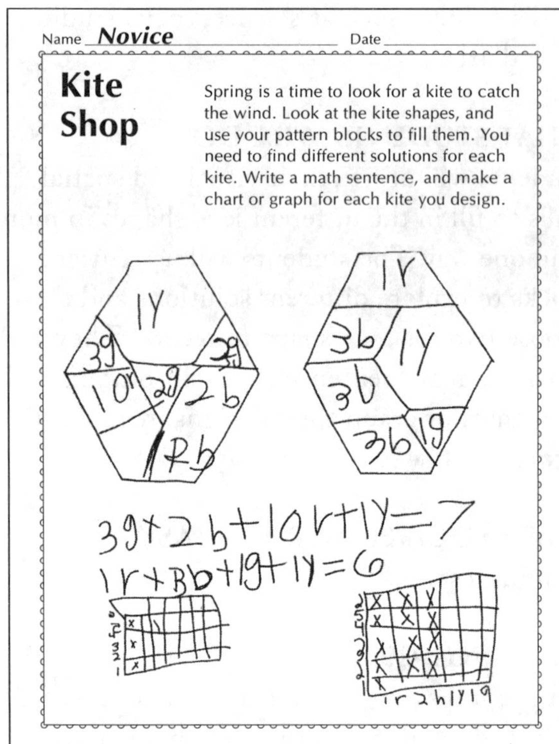

Name *Novice* Date

Kite Shop

Spring is a time to look for a kite to catch the wind. Look at the kite shapes, and use your pattern blocks to fill them. You need to find different solutions for each kite. Write a math sentence, and make a chart or graph for each kite you design.

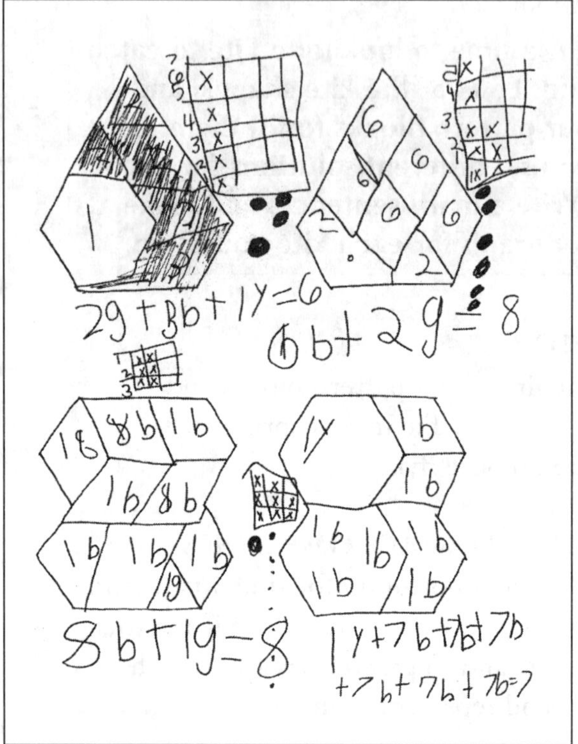

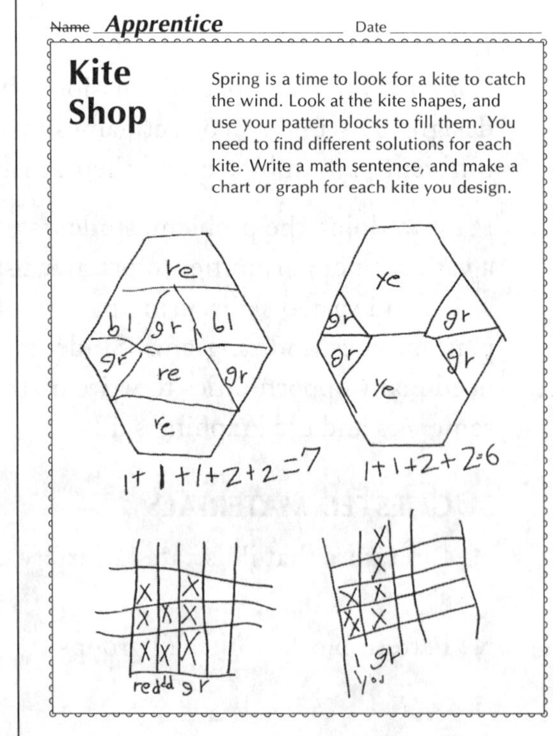

Name *Apprentice* Date

Kite Shop

Spring is a time to look for a kite to catch the wind. Look at the kite shapes, and use your pattern blocks to fill them. You need to find different solutions for each kite. Write a math sentence, and make a chart or graph for each kite you design.

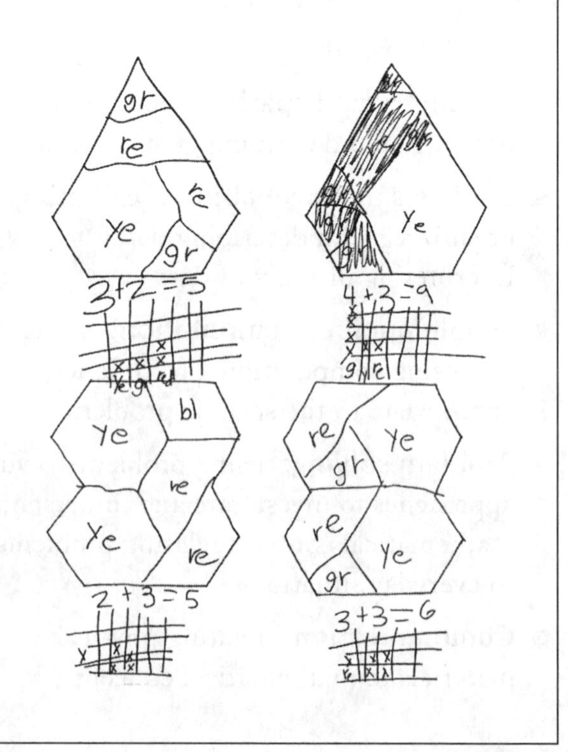

POSSIBLE SOLUTIONS

This task lends itself to several possible solutions for each kite shape. In their solutions, the blocks must be labeled by color, and children must include an appropriate mathematical sentence for each design, as well as a graph or chart to show their interpretation of data. Some students might chart each design or combine some of them, which would illustrate extensions of mathematical ideas.

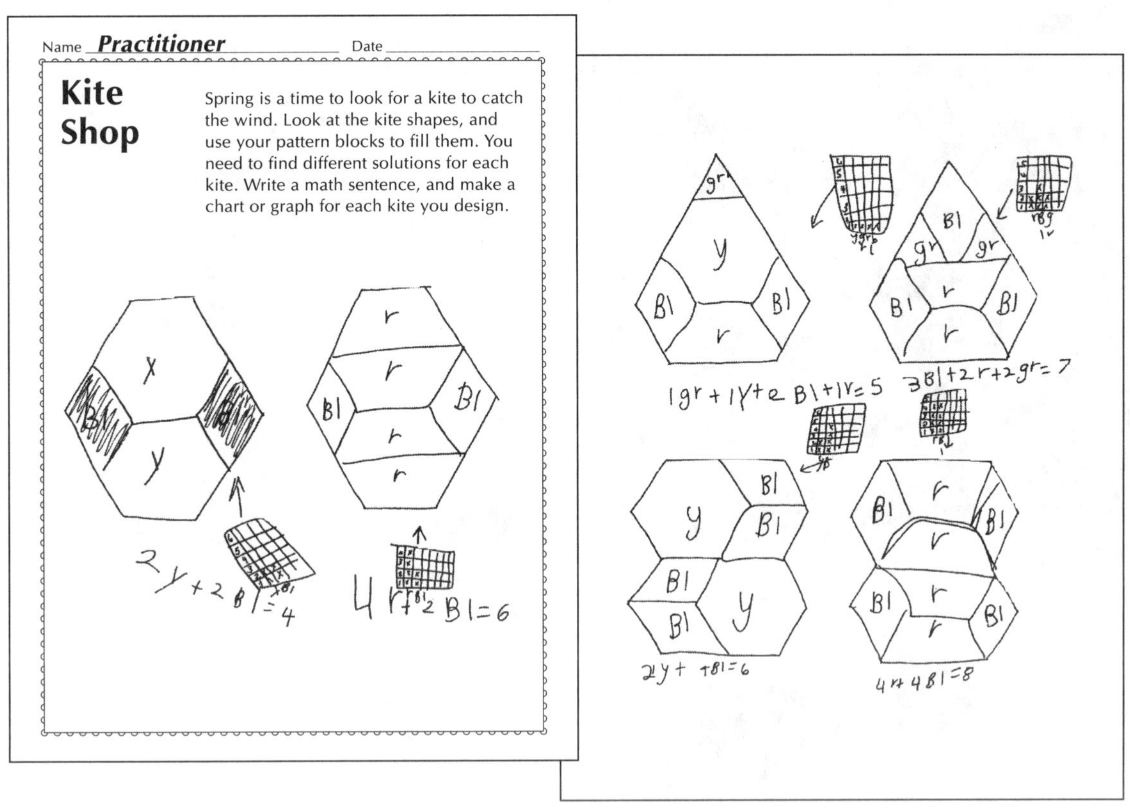

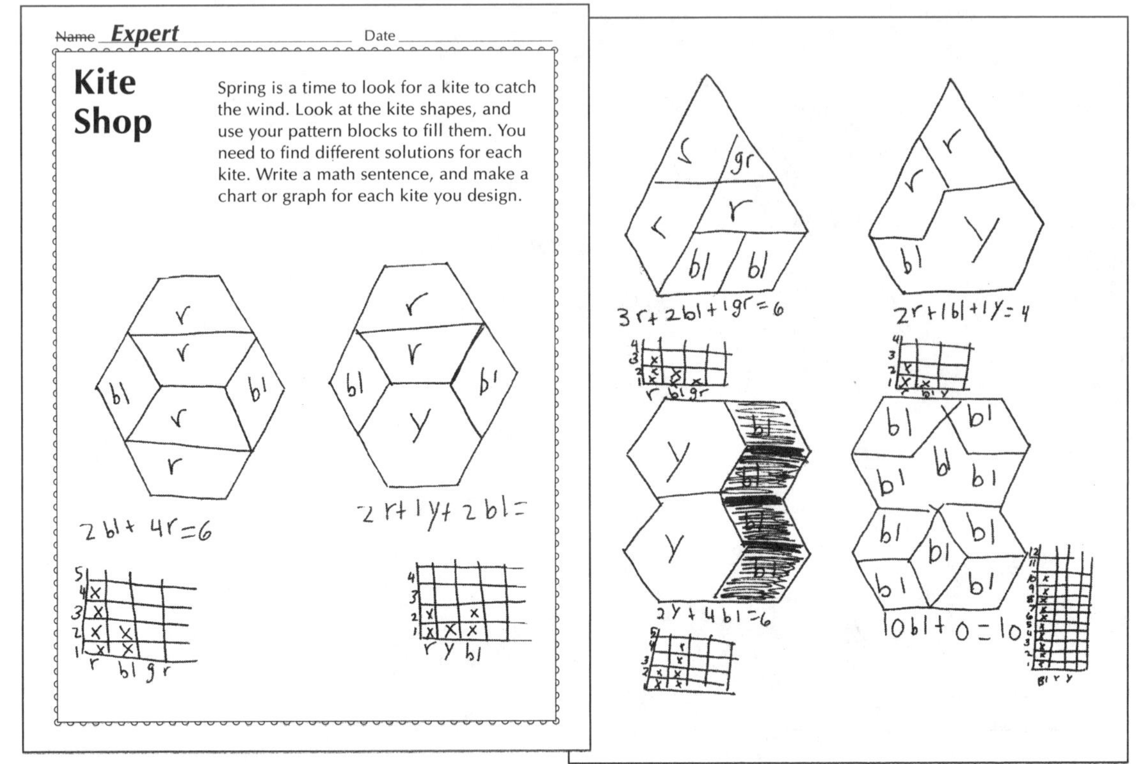

Name ______________________ Date ______________

Farmyard

A farmer saw:

4 heads

10 legs

3 tails

What animals did he see? Please show and explain your work, using pictures, numbers, and words.

Farmyard

Teaching Tips Page

Grade Level: K–2

THE TASK
A farmer saw:
4 heads
10 legs
3 tails
What animals did he see? Please show and explain your work, using pictures, numbers, and words.

WHEN TO USE

This performance task should be given after your addition unit is taught and students have had experience with problem-solving activities.

WHAT THIS TASK ACCOMPLISHES

It will show children's mathematical thinking and identify those who have a conceptual understanding of combining numbers in many different ways to equal a given sum. It will offer insights into problem solving in a more general way, and it will allow for creativity.

CONCEPTS ASSESSED AND SKILLS DEVELOPED

- The problem-solving process
- Communication (diagram and/or verbal response)
- Reasoning and decision making
- Recognition and use of patterns
- Number sense
- Addition

WHAT STUDENTS WILL DO

A student will independently solve this problem on the task sheet. If more room is needed, the child may use the back and/or another sheet. The child is encouraged to use diagrams, numbers, and words to indicate mathematical thinking. There are many solutions, and if more than one solution is found, the child is encouraged to show all solutions.

TEACHING TIPS

Introduce the problem by talking about a farm. What kinds of animals live on a farm? Brainstorm a list of farm animals. What do some of the animals look like? Say to students: The farmer in this problem doesn't have a very good view of the animals. All he can see is 4 heads, 10 legs, and 3 tails. Our job is to help him decide what animals he sees.

POSSIBLE SOLUTIONS

This is an open-ended activity that has many possible solutions.

Authors: **Darlene Johnson** and **Sandra Silverman** teach at Oceanview Elementary School in Huntington Beach, California.

Name ______________________________ Date __________________

Field Trip

A class is planning transportation for a field trip.

Cars can take 4 passengers.

Vans can take 6 passengers.

There are 24 students in the class.

How many cars and vans are necessary to take the whole class? Please show and explain your work, using pictures, numbers, and words. Show as many solutions as you can.

Field Trip

Teaching Tips Page

Grade Level: K–2

THE TASK

A class is planning transportation for a field trip.

Cars can take 4 passengers.
Vans can take 6 passengers.
There are 24 students in the class.

How many cars and vans are necessary to take the whole class? Please explain your work, using pictures, numbers, and words. Show as many solutions as you can.

WHEN TO USE

This problem should be given after your addition unit has been taught.

WHAT THIS TASK ACCOMPLISHES

It will identify students who have a conceptual understanding of combining numbers in many different ways to equal a given sum.

CONCEPTS ASSESSED AND SKILLS DEVELOPED

- The problem-solving process
- Communication (diagram and/or verbal response)
- Reasoning and decision making
- Recognition and use of patterns
- Number sense
- Addition

WHAT STUDENTS WILL DO

Students will independently solve this problem on the attached task sheet. If more room is needed, the child may use the back and/or another sheet. The child is encouraged to use diagrams, numbers, and words to indicate his mathematical thinking. There are several solutions, and if more than one is found, the child is encouraged to show all solutions.

TEACHING TIPS

Set the stage for this activity by talking about going on a field trip, without using a bus. (For example: "Today we'll pretend we're going on a field trip. We don't have a bus, but we do have cars and vans. Cars can take 4 passengers, and vans can take 6 passengers. Our job is to decide just how many cars and vans to bring. We're only counting 24 students. We don't count drivers or teachers in the solution."

A Practitioner may be able to clearly identify a correct solution to this task. The Expert will clearly show some organization in his/her solution to be sure nearly all possible combinations of cars and vans are used. In addition, the Expert will use accurate and clear mathematical representation.

POSSIBLE SOLUTIONS

4 vans

6 cars

2 vans and 3 cars

Name ____________________ Date ____________________

Flags

Using three colors—red, blue, and white—in a vertical stripe pattern, how many different flags can you make? Each flag must use all three colors but must be different from the others.

Flags

Teaching Tips Page

Grade Level: K-2

THE TASK
Using three colors—red, blue, and white—in a vertical stripe pattern, how many different flags can you make? Each flag must use all three colors but must be different from the others.

WHEN TO USE
After teaching a unit on patterns and combinations

CONCEPTS ASSESSED AND SKILLS DEVELOPED
- Problem solving
- Reasoning
- Communicating
- Patterning
- Combinations

WHAT STUDENTS WILL DO
Some students use the guess-and-check strategy. They draw a flag and check to see if they used that combination before. Other students guess-and-check and then see patterns that help to make other combinations. A few students organize their approach by color—they find all the combinations starting with white, then blue, then red.

Let's look at what Susan took into consideration before she presented Flags to her class.

THE CONTEXT
In social studies, we were studying different cultures and countries and their flags. In math, we were classifying and sorting different attributes of flags. We had also been doing a good deal of work with two- and three-color patterns.

TIME REQUIRED FOR THE TASK
About a half hour

SETUP AND MATERIALS
I used the French flag as the model for the problem. Make a sheet with two rows of 4 blank flags in the same design as the French flag. Hand out sheets and red, white, and blue crayons to students.

POSSIBLE SOLUTIONS
red, white, blue
red, blue, white
white, red, blue
white, blue, red
blue, red, white
blue, white, red

Author: **Susan Nellen** is a first-grade teacher at the Marion Cross School in Norwich, Vermont.

Name ______________________ Date ______________

In Line

Five students are going on a treasure hunt. They need to line up with a girl as the line leader and a boy as the line follower. There are three girls and two boys. Show how many different ways they could line up and still follow the rules. Write a key so that we know what code you have used to show girls and boys. Your code may have shapes, colors, numbers, letters/words, symbols, or diagrams.

In Line

Teaching Tips Page

Grade Level: K–2

THE TASK

Five students are going on a treasure hunt. They need to line up with a girl as the line leader and a boy as the line follower. There are three girls and two boys. Show how many different ways they could line up and still follow the rules. Write a key so that we know what code you have used to show girls and boys. Your code may have shapes, colors, numbers, letters/words, symbols, or diagrams.

WHEN TO USE

After students have had experience organizing information

WHAT THIS TASK ACCOMPLISHES

It provides several solutions. Students need to create a key and use it appropriately. They need to organize possibilities using trial-and-error or by recognizing the solutions and how they are organized.

CONCEPTS ASSESSED AND SKILLS DEVELOPED

- Problem solving
- Organization
- Making and using a key
- Reasoning

THE CONTEXT

Lining up is a big event in my classroom. Students are always problem solving ways to line up on their own. While doing the problem we discussed possible ways to code girls and boys. Several students suggested using pink for girls and blue for boys. Others suggested long hair for girls and short hair for boys. Another suggested dresses for girls and pants for boys. When we were going over the solutions, we discussed sexism and stereotypes for about thirty minutes. To explain sexism, we compared it to racism, which led to a huge discussion of Martin Luther King, Jr.

TIME REQUIRED FOR THE TASK

15–20 minutes

TEACHING TIPS

Clarify that one code should be used for all of the solutions found. Have children generate a list of code possibilities.

SUGGESTED MATERIALS

Some students may wish to use manipulatives to try their possibilities before they write them.

POSSIBLE SOLUTIONS

g=girl and b=boy

gbggb

gggbb

ggbgb

Author: **Susan Nellen** is a first-grade teacher the Marion Cross School in Norwich, Vermont.

Name ______________________ Date ______________

Pentomino

Use the three pentominoes that are provided to make as many different shapes with twelve sides or less. Use the following three shapes:

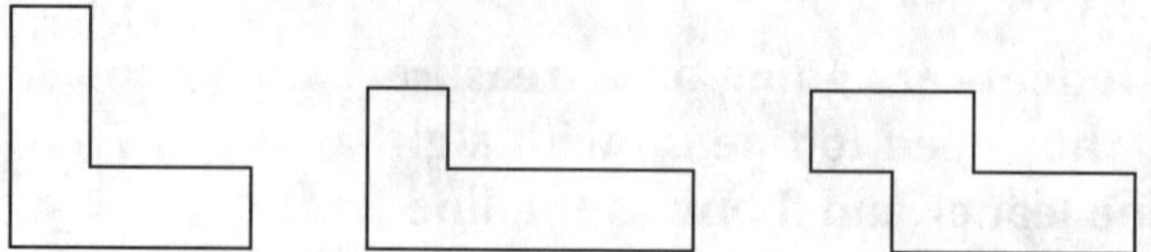

Pentomino

Teaching Tips Page

Grade Level: K–2

THE TASK

Use the three pentominoes that are provided to make as many different shapes with twelve sides or less. Use the following three shapes:

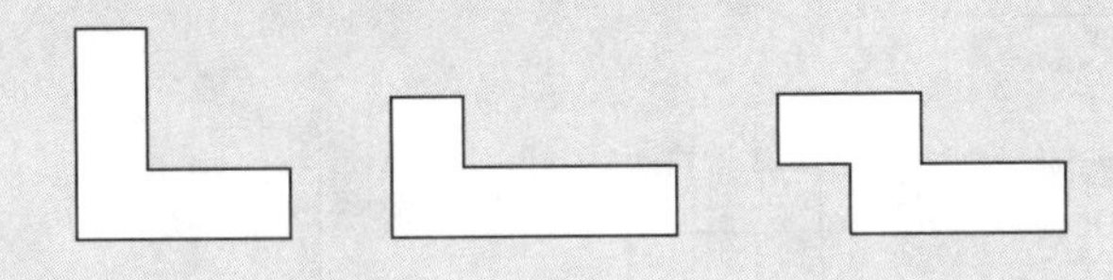

WHEN TO USE

After teaching a unit on estimation, shapes, and geometry

WHAT THIS TASK ACCOMPLISHES

Counting sides of geometric shapes

Turning, flipping, and sliding pieces to make shapes

Tracing

CONCEPTS ASSESSED AND SKILLS DEVELOPED

- Estimation
- Geometry and spatial problem solving
- Problem solving
- Communication
- Reasoning
- Connections

WHAT STUDENTS WILL DO

Make hollow shapes or pictures with the pieces

Use the same shapes several ways in the same solution

Make a shape with the pentominoes, count the sides, and trace the pieces if the shape fits the rule

Make a shape, trace the pieces, and count afterward

Make a shape, and trace just the outside so that the solution isn't clear

Include the number of sides on each pentomino, even when they aren't on the outside of the shape

Use only two of the pentominoes

When recording the sides, skip sides or count a side twice if two pieces meet on that side

Make shapes without the individual shapes traced and without numbers

Erase one of the pieces, and move it to a place that creates fewer sides

Put the pieces corner to corner, creating extra sides

TIME REQUIRED FOR THE TASK

20–30 minutes

TEACHING TIPS

Sort the pentomino sets ahead of time so that each student has the three pentominoes.

For the second half of first grade and for second grade, have the students find the three pentominoes.

Have kids play with a few pattern blocks to make shapes with as many or as few sides as they can.

Find shapes around the room with a given number of sides.

Identify the number of sides in shapes around the room.

Remind students to show solutions with tracing each pentomino.

With older or more advanced kids, have them try making shapes with the maximum number of sides being between 8–10.

SUGGESTED MATERIALS

- ❋ A set of pentominoes for each student so that she/he can have the same three pentominoes.
- ❋ Pencils

POSSIBLE SOLUTIONS

These are some solutions that a teacher came up with:

Author: **Cindy Pierce** is a first-grade teacher at the Marion Cross School in Norwich, Vermont.

Name ______________________ Date ______________

Six-Pack of Soda

I often buy cans of soda in a six-pack. If I buy two six-packs of soda each week, how many cans will I buy in a month to recycle? How many six-packs will that be?

Six-Pack of Soda

Teaching Tips Page

Grade Level: K–2

THE TASK
I often buy cans of soda in a six-pack. If I buy two six-packs of soda each week, how many cans will I buy in a month to recycle? How many six-packs will that be?

WHEN TO USE
After students are familiar with counting, grouping, and patterns

WHAT THIS TASK ACCOMPLISHES
Children work with the number set of six, and group objects by the dozen. It also requires that students change the month into weeks, and it asks children to organize their information to devise a diagram that solves the problem.

THE CONTEXT
My first graders do a lot of activities that emphasize the impact of packaging and recycling on our Earth through an environmental theme. The children investigate the paper, glass, plastic, and other materials their families throw away every day. They also learn about the dangers of plastic six-pack rings to wildlife.

WHAT STUDENTS WILL DO
Students should represent the cans in groups of six rings by each week and come up with a total number of cans to recycle, and the number of six-packs purchased.

TEACHING TIPS
Invite the class to discuss how to change a month into weeks. After this, give each group a plastic six-pack wrapper to examine, and a six-pack of soda to refer to, if needed. Make small tubs of rainbow tiles available for a tactile approach.

TIME REQUIRED FOR THE TASK
30–45 minutes

Author: **Sandy Haddock** is a primary teacher at Bristol Elementary School in Bristol, Vermont.

Name *Novice* Date

Six-Pack of Soda

I often buy cans of soda in a six-pack. If I buy two six-packs of soda each week, how many cans will I buy in a month to recycle? How many six-packs will that be?

8 3

24 can

I buy cans of soda in a six-pack. If I buy 2 six-packs each week, how many will I buy in a month to recycle?

4 rac a wnc

Need short caption for here please.

This student started to use helpful mathematical procedure but didn't carry it through. Even though she has an understanding of the concept of 6, and verbally stated this while using the models provided, she did not represent this in the diagram and was unable to get close to a solution.

Name *Apprentice* Date

Six-Pack of Soda

I often buy cans of soda in a six-pack. If I buy two six-packs of soda each week, how many cans will I buy in a month to recycle? How many six-packs will that be?

Week1 Week2 Week 3 Week4

4 cans for am month anothere 4 and a nother and a nothe an a nothe

I buy cans of soda in a six-pack. If I buy 2 six-packs each week, how many will I buy in a month to recycle?

this Math is hrde I rote week 1 and week 2 and week 3 an week 4 and then drew the cans

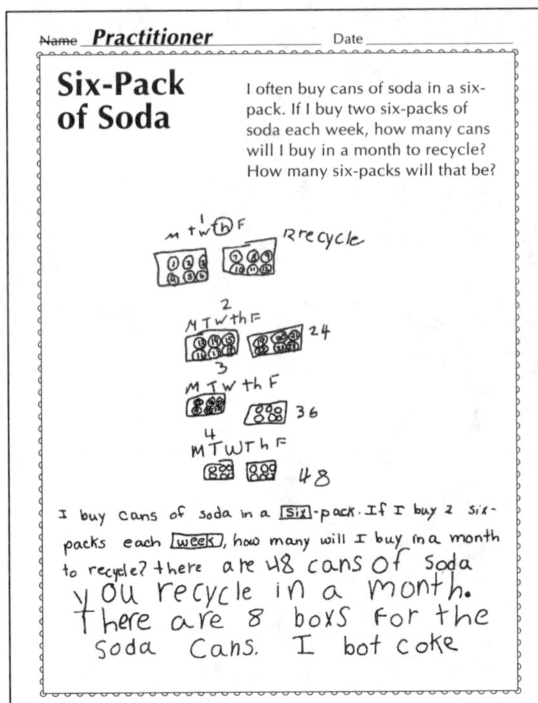

Name *Practitioner* Date

Six-Pack of Soda

I often buy cans of soda in a six-pack. If I buy two six-packs of soda each week, how many cans will I buy in a month to recycle? How many six-packs will that be?

1 M T W Th F 12 recycle

2 M T W th F 24

3 M T W th F 36

4 M T W T h F 48

I buy cans of soda in a six-pack. If I buy 2 six-packs each week, how many will I buy in a month to recycle? there are 48 cans of soda you recycle in a month. there are 8 boxs for the soda cans. I bot coke

This student clearly had a broad understanding of the task. He used a strategy for the calendar component and accurately represented the number of six-packs weekly. The solution shows effective mathematical reasoning, and the explanation is clear.

This student has a deep understanding of the problem and uses an effective strategy to come to a solution of 48 cans. She has a clear concept of grouping by six, and the 4 weeks in a month. The mathematical notation is appropriate and detailed.

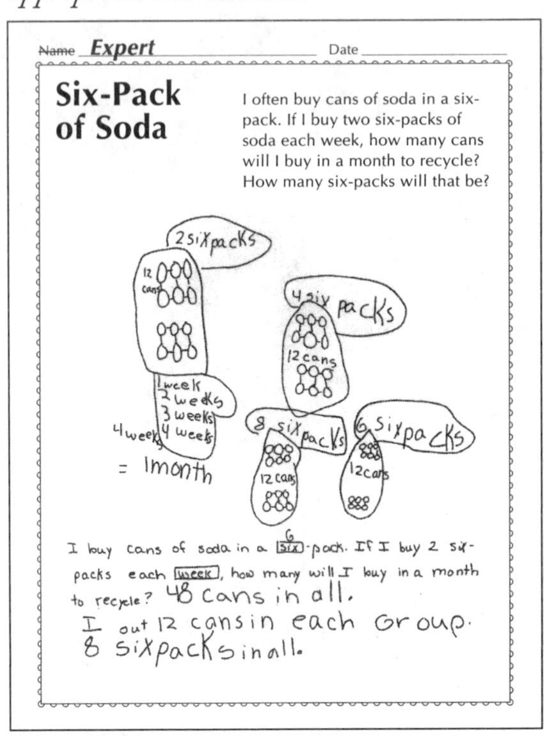

Name *Expert* Date

Six-Pack of Soda

I often buy cans of soda in a six-pack. If I buy two six-packs of soda each week, how many cans will I buy in a month to recycle? How many six-packs will that be?

2 sixpacks 12 cans; 4 six packs 12 cans; 8 sixpacks 12 cans; 6 sixpacks 12 cans

1 week 2 weeks 3 weeks 4 weeks; 4 weeks = 1 month

I buy cans of soda in a six-pack. If I buy 2 six-packs each week, how many will I buy in a month to recycle? 48 cans in all. I put 12 cans in each group. 8 sixpacks in all.

Name ______________________ Date ______________

Darts

Tony threw 6 darts and scored 32 points. Where did his darts land?

Darts

Teaching Tips Page

Grade Level: K–2

THE TASK
Tony threw 6 darts and scored 32 points. Where did his darts land?

WHEN TO USE
After teaching a unit on addition

WHAT THIS TASK ACCOMPLISHES
It shows students' ability to solve problems in a different context and explain their results, while adding more than one number.

THE CONTEXT
Students had learned various approaches to adding more than one number. The students were comfortable with the mechanics of the problem but had difficulty illustrating it or explaining their reasoning.

WHAT STUDENTS WILL DO
Students will try to arrive at 32, using the four given values. Most will use a guess-and-check approach to this problem. If students have not had experience with problem solving, they will have trouble explaining their reasoning.

TIME REQUIRED FOR THE TASK
Introduce and discuss for about 10 minutes so that the students will be familiar with a dart board and scoring system. Provide about 15 or 20 minutes longer to solve and explain.

TEACHING TIPS
Display a dart board. Introduce students to different approaches of adding one number. They should also be familiar with solving number sentences, labeling answers, illustrating problems, and solving a problem in more than one way before the problem is given as an assessment.

Author: **Cynthia McWilliams** teaches second grade at Shiloh Elementary School in Lithonia, Georgia.

Name ______________________ Date ______________

Bowls of Apples

There are 16 apples to put into bowls. Each bowl must have the same number of apples. Show how you could put the apples into bowls.

Bowls of Apples

Teaching Tips Page

Grade Level: K–2

THE TASK
There are 16 apples to put into bowls. Each bowl must have the same number of apples. Show how you could put the apples into bowls.

WHEN TO USE

This is an open-response problem because there is more than one solution. It shows students' understanding of number sense and patterns. The problem allows students to investigate division and fractions.

WHAT THIS TASK ACCOMPLISHES

It offers a concrete assessment of students' understanding of fractions and division.

WHAT STUDENTS WILL DO

By using diagrams and manipulatives as they solve this problem, students will be able to demonstrate their understanding of fractions. They will also show their ability to solve problems. Some students will find one solution and stop, while others will show several different solutions.

TIME REQUIRED FOR THE TASK

The time used solving this problem will vary. Some students will take longer to get started, while others will pursue several solutions. About 30 minutes should be adequate.

TEACHING TIPS

Students who do this problem should have some knowledge of the concept of sharing. It would be helpful if they had some concrete experience with a similar problem before the assessment. However, if their experience is more limited, it may demonstrate their problem-solving abilities and innate sense of fractions and division.

Author: **Judy Cole** has taught first grade in Colorado for thirty years.

Name ______________________________ Date ____________________

Tollbooth

There are 3 ways to get to Candy Land. Snickers Street has 4 tollbooths, and each one costs 10 cents. Licorice Lane has 7 tollbooths, and each one costs 5 cents. Reeses Road has 3 tollbooths, and each one costs 20 cents. Which route will be the cheapest? How do you know?

Tollbooth

Teaching Tips Page

Grade Level: K–2

THE TASK

There are 3 ways to get to Candy Land. Snickers Street has 4 tollbooths, and each one costs 10 cents. Licorice Lane has 7 tollbooths, and each one costs 5 cents. Reeses Road has 3 tollbooths, and each one costs 20 cents. Which route will be the cheapest? How do you know?

WHEN TO USE

After teaching students about money, addition, and counting

CONCEPTS ASSESSED AND SKILLS DEVELOPED

- **Problem solving:** Use problem-solving approaches to investigate math content
- Develop and apply strategies to solve a variety of problems
- **Communication:** Relate physical materials to mathematical ideas
- Clarify thinking about mathematical situations
- **Reasoning:** Justify answers and solution processes
- **Connections:** Integrate computation with measurement
- **Number sense and numeration**: Count by 5s, 10s and 2s. More could mean less, and less could mean more
- **Measurement:** Knowledge of money
- **Concept of whole number computation and operations:** Addition/Multiplication
- Develop operation sense

WHAT THIS TASK ACCOMPLISHES

It asks students to balance information to solve the problem. They can use diagrams, words, numbers, and equations to solve the problem. They need to develop strategies to add large numbers (count by 5s and 10s, use multiplication, etc.).

WHAT STUDENTS WILL DO

Some students will guess and figure out the total for that choice. Others will use multiplication. Some will use addition for all three. Some students will choose the one that has the cheapest tolls, while others will choose the one with the least number of tolls. Some will guess and explain with random reasoning.

TIME REQUIRED FOR THE TASK

20–35 minutes

TEACHING TIPS

Write the important information for each toll booth (Snickers St. = 4 tolls, 10 cents each) on chart paper to review with students.

Define the word *cheapest.*

Discuss tolls and their purpose.

Remind them that it will cost them however much at each tollbooth and that it will accumulate by the end of the road.

SUGGESTED MATERIALS

- Paper, pencils, real or fake coins

POSSIBLE SOLUTIONS

There is one solution.

Licorice Lane would be the cheapest because seven tolls at 5 cents apiece would cost 35 cents. Snickers Street would cost 40 cents (4 tolls at 10 cents apiece). Reeses Road would cost 60 cents (3 tolls at 20 cents apiece).

Author: **Cindy Pierce** teaches at the Marion Cross School, in Norwich, Vermont.

Name *Novice* Date

Tollbooth There are 3 ways to get to Candy Land. Snickers Street has 4 tollbooths, and each one costs 10 cents. Licorice Lane has 7 tollbooths, and each one costs 5 cents. Reeses Road has 3 tollbooths, and each one costs 20 cents. Which route will be the cheapest? How do you know?

BY CAS IT IS FAIIE SANS AND IT IS NAT FARE MAG MANE IT IS FAIIF PANEAS (pennies)

T: Which one? B: Licorice Lane T: How do you know it cheapest?

This student did not understand that the cost would accumulate after going through a number of tolls. The student decided that the least expensive toll meant it was the cheapest route. This student's diagram showed 1 toll booth and explained in words that 5 cents is 5 pennies.

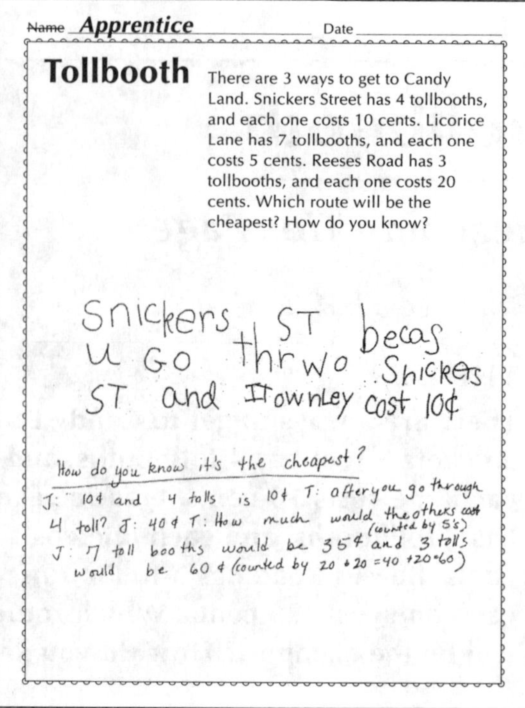

Name *Apprentice* Date

Tollbooth There are 3 ways to get to Candy Land. Snickers Street has 4 tollbooths, and each one costs 10 cents. Licorice Lane has 7 tollbooths, and each one costs 5 cents. Reeses Road has 3 tollbooths, and each one costs 20 cents. Which route will be the cheapest? How do you know?

Snickers ST becas u Go thrwo Snickers ST and Itownley cost 10¢

How do you know it's the cheapest?

J: 10¢ and 4 tolls is 10¢ T: after you go through 4 toll? J: 40¢ T: How much would the others cost J: 7 toll booths would be 35¢ (counted by 5's) and 3 tolls would be 60¢ (counted by 20 + 20 = 40 + 20 = 60)

This student understood most of the problem but confused some of the information. A low cost and a low number of tolls seemed to be a better choice than choosing one with a high number of tolls but a low fare. The student was capable of coming up with a sum, but needed prompting to understand that going through the tolls would eventually add up by the end.

This student understood the problem and was able to use addition to get the answer. She could explain the solution and write the results. The student is able to communicate using a variety of terms, symbols, and notations.

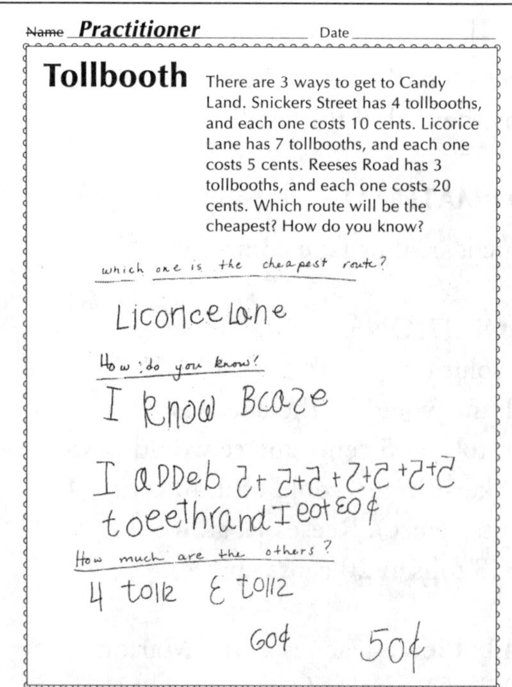

Name *Practitioner* Date

Tollbooth There are 3 ways to get to Candy Land. Snickers Street has 4 tollbooths, and each one costs 10 cents. Licorice Lane has 7 tollbooths, and each one costs 5 cents. Reeses Road has 3 tollbooths, and each one costs 20 cents. Which route will be the cheapest? How do you know?

which one is the cheapest route?

LiconceLane

How do you know?

I know Bcaze

I aDDeb 5+5+5+5+5+5+5 toeethrand I eot 50¢

How much are the others?

4 tolle & tolle

60¢ 50¢

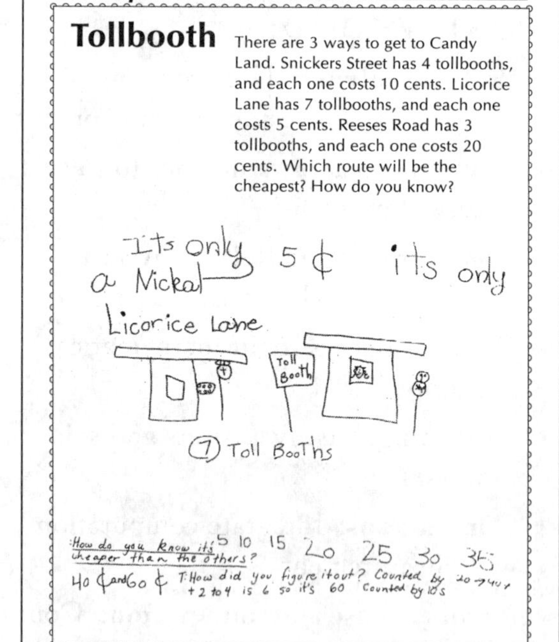

Name *Expert* Date

Tollbooth There are 3 ways to get to Candy Land. Snickers Street has 4 tollbooths, and each one costs 10 cents. Licorice Lane has 7 tollbooths, and each one costs 5 cents. Reeses Road has 3 tollbooths, and each one costs 20 cents. Which route will be the cheapest? How do you know?

Its only 5¢ its only a Nickal Licorice Lane

Toll Booth

(7) Toll BooThs

How do you know it's cheaper than the others? 5 10 15 20 25 30 35

40¢ and 60¢ T: How did you figure it out? Counted by 10s +2 to 4 is 6 so it's 60 Counted by 20→40

This student was able to show and explain the solution in at least two ways (addition, and counting by 5s, 10s, and 20s). The student could add lower numbers (2 for 20, 4 for 40) and translate them correctly by adding a zero after reaching a sum. The student was able to communicate using terms and symbols, and attempted to create a diagram.

Name ______________________ Date ______________

Sink or Float

Which objects do you think will float, and which do you think will sink? Be sure to make predictions, and categorize the objects that float and the objects that sink. What do you think they have in common, or how are they different?

Sink or Float

Teaching Tips Page

Grade Level: K–2

THE TASK
Which objects do you think will float, and which do you think will sink? Be sure to make predictions, and categorize the objects that float and the objects that sink. What do you think they have in common, or how are they different?

WHEN TO USE

After teaching students about comparison, estimation, and patterns

WHAT THIS TASK ACCOMPLISHES

It makes use of these skills: observing, classifying, recording data, comparing weight and size, and estimating.

THE CONTEXT

This problem was part of an investigation into things that float on and things that sink in water. We have been investigating water for over a month as one of our science units. The children had compared water to sand and rice, investigated how things look through and on water, observed how sand and oil mix with water, found how things absorb and repel water, and observed the movement of water droplets with food coloring.

WHAT STUDENTS WILL DO

In solving this problem, the students were encouraged to test as many materials as possible, to observe if they sank or floated, and to determine if some materials made them question either category. We spent time predicting what some of the different objects might do before starting the testing situation. A collection of objects that sink and float were provided for the students to select. Six tubs of water were placed around the room for the students to use. The students were encouraged to sort the objects in some way after they had tested each. I asked them to use their math skills and individual writing skills to label everything they did in a way that made sense to them.

TIME REQUIRED FOR THE TASK

The students worked on this problem 60 minutes before lunch break and 30 minutes after lunch/recess time. It was split this way on purpose so they would observe any changes in the materials over time.

SUGGESTED MATERIALS

A selection of items such as:

- cork, washers, Styrofoam cups, wooden wheels, dominoes, sponges, paper clips, a Ping-Pong ball, marble stone, clay, pennies, paper, paper towels, balloons, erasers, felt, buttons, a unifix cube, a clothespin, a straw, and a plastic cup
- 6 tubs of water

Author: **Sandy Haddock** is a first-grade teacher at Bristol Elementary School in Bristol, Vermont.

Name ______________________________ Date ____________________

7 Coins

Mom has 7 coins in her pocket. She has at least one of each coin: quarter, dime, nickel, and penny. How much money could she have? Please show and explain your work, using pictures, numbers, and words. Show as many solutions as you can.

7 Coins

Teaching Tips Page

Grade Level: K–2

THE TASK
Mom has 7 coins in her pocket. She has at least one of each coin: quarter, dime, nickel, and penny. How much money could she have? Please show and explain your work, using pictures, numbers, and words. Show as many solutions as you can.

WHEN TO USE

After teaching a unit on money

WHAT THIS TASK ACCOMPLISHES

It will identify students who have a conceptual understanding of coin recognition, value, and exchange properties.

CONCEPTS ASSESSED AND SKILLS DEVELOPED

- The problem-solving process
- Communication (diagram and/or verbal response)
- Coin recognition
- Coin value
- Money counting
- Money exchange

WHAT STUDENTS WILL DO

Students will independently solve this problem on the attached task sheet. If more room is needed, the child may use the back and/or another sheet. The child may trace around coins, if desired. The child is encouraged to use diagrams, numbers, and words to indicate his mathematical thinking. There are many solutions, and if more than one solution is found, the child is encouraged to show all solutions.

TEACHING TIPS

Set the stage for this activity by talking about how people, especially adults, carry a lot of coins in their pockets. (For example: "Let's pretend we're going shopping with Mom. We know she has some coins in her pocket and may have enough money to buy a treat. But we don't know how much money she has. All she will tell us is that it's 7 coins! We have to figure out how much money she might have."

A Practitioner may be able to clearly identify many solutions to this task, but they may appear in a more random order. The Expert will clearly show some organization in the solution to be sure nearly all possible combinations of coins are used.

POSSIBLE SOLUTIONS

4 quarters, 1 dime, 1 nickel, 1 penny = $1.16

3 quarters, 2 dimes, 1 nickel, 1 penny = $1.01

3 quarters, 1 dime, 2 nickels, 1 penny = $.96

3 quarters, 1 dime, 1 nickel, 2 pennies = $.92

2 quarters, 3 dimes, 1 nickel, 1 penny = $.86

2 quarters, 2 dimes, 1 nickel, 2 pennies = $.77

2 quarters, 1 dime, 3 nickels, 1 penny = $.76

2 quarters, 1 dime, 2 nickels, 2 pennies = $.72

2 quarters, 1 dime, 1 nickel, 3 pennies = $.68

1 quarter, 4 dimes, 1 nickel, 1 penny = $.71

1 quarter, 3 dimes, 2 nickels, 1 penny = $.66

1 quarter, 3 dimes, 1 nickel, 2 pennies = $.62

1 quarter, 2 dimes, 3 nickels, 1 penny = $.61

1 quarter, 2 dimes, 2 nickels, 2 pennies = $.57

1 quarter, 2 dimes, 1 nickels, 3 pennies = $.53

1 quarter, 1 dime, 4 nickels, 1 penny = $.56

1 quarter, 1 dime, 3 nickels, 2 pennies = $.52

1 quarter, 1 dime, 2 nickels, 3 pennies = $.48

1 quarter, 1 dime, 1 nickel, 4 pennies = $.44

Author: **Katonah-Lewisboro Math Assessment Committee** from Katonah, New York

Name ______________________________ Date ____________________

The Fish Dilemma

There are 3 boats. There are 4 people fishing on each boat. Each person may catch up to 3 fish. How many fish could be caught? Show as many different ways to solve this problem as possible. For each solution you find, draw a picture, and explain it in numbers and words.

The Fish Dilemma

Teaching Tips Page

Grade Level: K–2

THE TASK

There are 3 boats. There are 4 people fishing on each boat. Each person may catch up to 3 fish. How many fish could be caught? Show as many different ways to solve this problem as possible. For each solution you find, draw a picture, and explain it in numbers and words.

WHEN TO USE

After teaching units on addition and combinations

WHAT THIS TASK ACCOMPLISHES

It will identify students who have a broad understanding of problem-solving strategies. It will also identify students who have an organizational approach to problem solving.

CONCEPTS ASSESSED AND SKILLS DEVELOPED

- Problem solving with multisteps
- Reasoning
- Communication
- Whole number operations
- Combinations

WHAT STUDENTS WILL DO

Students will independently solve this problem on the attached task sheet. If more room is needed, the child may use the back and/or another sheet. Graph paper may be used, if desired. Many students will draw diagrams, while others will make a chart of their findings. Many students will find the extremes—the most and least fish that can be caught.

TEACHING TIPS

Set the stage for children by talking about fishing. "Our task today is to determine how many fish could be caught if there are 3 fishing boats and 4 men fishing on each boat. Remember that each person is allowed to catch up to 3 fish."

A Practitioner may be able to clearly identify many solutions to this task. However, they may appear to be in a random order. The Expert will clearly show organization in his/her solution to show that nearly all possible solutions are found.

POSSIBLE SOLUTIONS

The maximum number of fish to be caught is 36.

The least number of fish that can be caught is 0.

Boat 1: 4 people per boat

3,3,3,3,
3,3,3,2
3,3,2,2
3,2,2,2
2,2,2,2
2,2,2,1
2,2,1,1
2,1,1,1
1,1,1,1
1,1,1,0
1,1,0,0
1,0,0,0
0,0,0,0

Boat 2: 4 people per boat

3,3,3,3
3,3,3,2
3,3,2,2
3,2,2,2
2,2,2,2
2,2,2,1
2,2,1,1
2,1,1,1
1,1,1,1
1,1,1,0
1,1,0,0

1,0,0,0
0,0,0,0

BOAT 3: 4 people per boat

3,3,3,3
3,3,3,2
3,3,2,2
3,2,2,2
2,2,2,2
2,2,2,1
2,2,1,1
2,1,1,1
1,1,1,1
1,1,1,0
1,1,0,0
1,0,0,0
0,0,0,0

EXEMPLARS RUBRIC

Level	Understanding	Strategies, Reasoning, Procedures	Communication
Novice (circled)	• There is no solution, or the solution has no relationship to the task. ✓ • Inappropriate concepts or procedures are used.	✓ No evidence of a strategy or procedure, or uses a strategy that does not help solve the problem. • No evidence of mathematical reasoning. • There were so many errors in mathematical procedure that the problem could not be solved.	✓ There is no explanation of the solution, the explanation cannot be understood or it is unrelated to the problem. ✓ There is no use or inappropriate use of mathematical representations (e.g., figures, diagrams, graphs, tables, etc.) ✓ There is no use, or mostly inappropriate use, of mathematical terminology and notation.
Apprentice	• The solution is not complete, indicating that parts of the problem are not understood.	• Uses a strategy that is partially useful, leading some way toward a solution, but not to a full solution of the problem. • Some evidence of mathematical reas… • Cou… math…	• There is an incomplete explanation; it may not be clearly presented. • There is some use of appropriate mathematical representation. …ology
Practitioner	• The solution shows that the student has a broad understanding of the problem and the major concepts necessary for its solution.	• Uses… the… • Uses… • Math… appr…	…ematical …minology
Expert	• The solution shows a deep understanding of the problem, including the ability to identify the appropriate mathematical concepts and the information necessary for its solution.	• Uses… strat… • Emp… • App… corr… the…	…ailing …s are … to infer …sed as a … the

Name *Novice* Date

The Fish Dilemma

There are 3 boats. There are 4 people fishing on each boat. Each person may catch up to 3 fish. How many fish could be caught? Show as many different ways to solve this problem as possible. For each solution you find, draw a picture, and explain it in numbers and words.

Build 3 boats. There are 4 people fishing on each boat. Each person may catch up to 3 fish. How many fish were caught?

3 boats 4 person. each person caught 1 fish h&f fish c 940fits

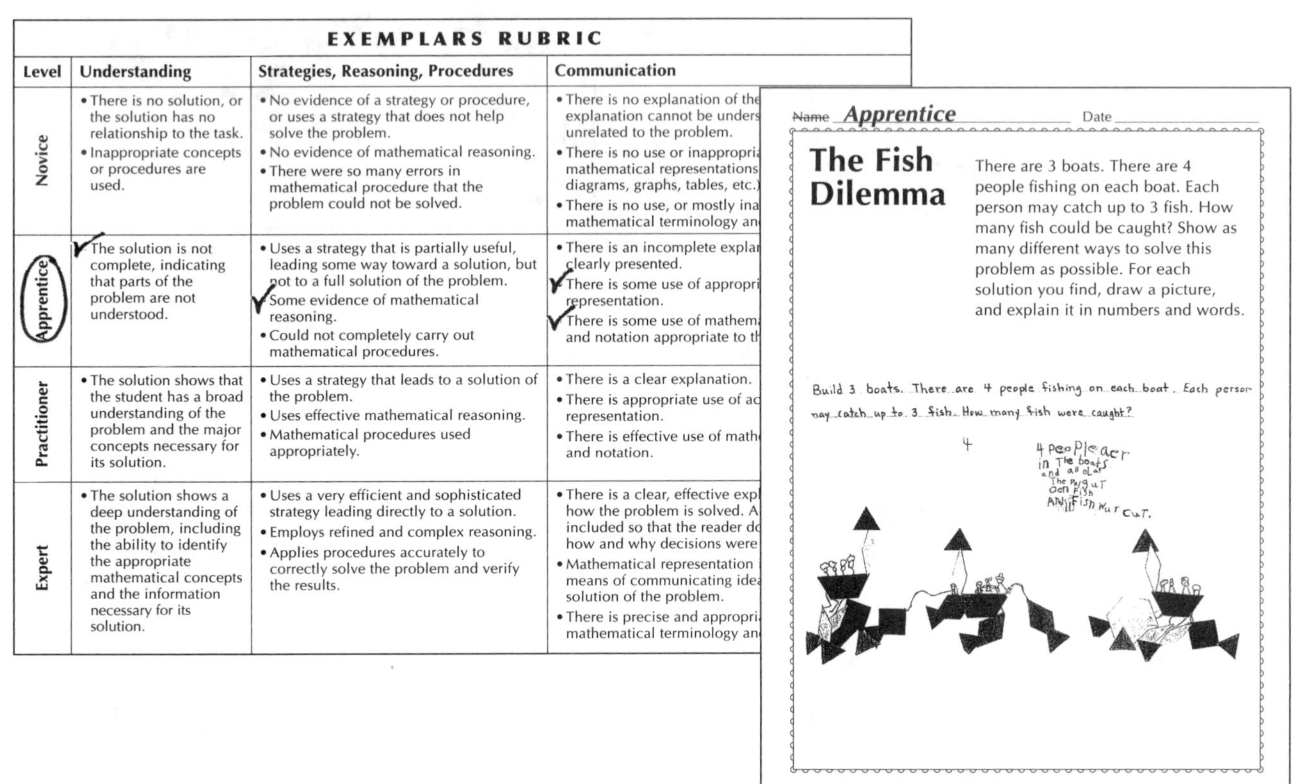

EXEMPLARS RUBRIC

Level	Understanding	Strategies, Reasoning, Procedures	Communication
Novice	• There is no solution, or the solution has no relationship to the task. • Inappropriate concepts or procedures are used.	• No evidence of a strategy or procedure, or uses a strategy that does not help solve the problem. • No evidence of mathematical reasoning. • There were so many errors in mathematical procedure that the problem could not be solved.	• There is no explanation of the… explanation cannot be unders… unrelated to the problem. • There is no use or inappropri… mathematical representations… diagrams, graphs, tables, etc.) • There is no use, or mostly ina… mathematical terminology an…
Apprentice (circled)	✓ The solution is not complete, indicating that parts of the problem are not understood.	• Uses a strategy that is partially useful, leading some way toward a solution, but not to a full solution of the problem. ✓ Some evidence of mathematical reasoning. • Could not completely carry out mathematical procedures.	• There is an incomplete explan… clearly presented. ✓ There is some use of appropri… representation. ✓ There is some use of mathem… and notation appropriate to th…
Practitioner	• The solution shows that the student has a broad understanding of the problem and the major concepts necessary for its solution.	• Uses a strategy that leads to a solution of the problem. • Uses effective mathematical reasoning. • Mathematical procedures used appropriately.	• There is a clear explanation. • There is appropriate use of ac… representation. • There is effective use of math… and notation.
Expert	• The solution shows a deep understanding of the problem, including the ability to identify the appropriate mathematical concepts and the information necessary for its solution.	• Uses a very efficient and sophisticated strategy leading directly to a solution. • Employs refined and complex reasoning. • Applies procedures accurately to correctly solve the problem and verify the results.	• There is a clear, effective exp… how the problem is solved. A… included so that the reader d… how and why decisions were… • Mathematical representation… means of communicating ide… solution of the problem. • There is precise and appropri… mathematical terminology an…

Name *Apprentice* Date

The Fish Dilemma

There are 3 boats. There are 4 people fishing on each boat. Each person may catch up to 3 fish. How many fish could be caught? Show as many different ways to solve this problem as possible. For each solution you find, draw a picture, and explain it in numbers and words.

Build 3 boats. There are 4 people fishing on each boat. Each person may catch up to 3 fish. How many fish were caught?

4

4 people ar in the boats and all of the people got fish and fish wur cut.

EXEMPLARS RUBRIC			
Level	**Understanding**	**Strategies, Reasoning, Procedures**	**Communication**
Novice	• There is no solution, or the solution has no relationship to the task. • Inappropriate concepts or procedures are used.	• No evidence of a strategy or procedure, or uses a strategy that does not help solve the problem. • No evidence of mathematical reasoning. • There were so many errors in mathematical procedure that the problem could not be solved.	• There is no explanation of the solution, the explanation cannot be understood or it is unrelated to the problem. • There is no use or inappropriate use of mathematical representations (e.g., figures, diagrams, graphs, tables, etc.) • There is no use, or mostly inappropriate use, of mathematical terminology and notation.
Apprentice	• The solution is not complete, indicating that parts of the problem are not understood.	• Uses a strategy that is partially useful, leading some way toward a solution, but not to a full solution of the problem. • Some evidence of mathematical reasoning. • Could not completely carry out mathematical procedures.	• There is an incomplete explanation; it may not be clearly presented. • There is some use of appropriate mathematical representation. • There is some use of mathematical terminology and notation appropriate to the problem.
Practitioner	✓ The solution shows that the student has a broad understanding of the problem and the major concepts necessary for its solution.	✓ Uses a strategy that leads to a solution of the problem. ✓ Uses effective mathematical reasoning. ✓ Mathematical procedures used appropriately.	• There is a clear explanation. ✓ There is appropriate use of accurate mathematical representation. ✓ There is effective use of mathematical terminology and notation.
Expert	• The solution shows a deep understanding of the problem, including the ability to identify the appropriate mathematical concepts and the information necessary for its solution.	• Uses a very efficient and sophisticated strategy leading directly to a solution. • Employs refined and complex reasoning. • Applies procedures accurately to correctly solve the problem and verify the results.	• There is a clear, effective explanation detailing how the problem is solved. All of the steps are included so that the reader does not need to infer how and why decisions were made. • Mathematical represent... means of communicati... solution of the problem... • There is precise and ap... mathematical terminolo...

Name *Practitioner* Date

The Fish Dilemma

There are 3 boats. There are 4 people fishing on each boat. Each person may catch up to 3 fish. How many fish could be caught? Show as many different ways to solve this problem as possible. For each solution you find, draw a picture, and explain it in numbers and words.

Name ______________________ Date ______________

Witches' Troubles

There are 20 witches who need a ride on a broomstick.
There are 8 brooms.
No more than 4 witches can fit on a broom, and no fewer than 2 witches can ride on a broom. Show and explain with pictures, words, and numbers how you would place all 20 witches on 8 brooms.

Witches' Troubles

Teaching Tips Page

Grade Level: K–2

THE TASK

There are 20 witches who need a ride on a broomstick.
There are 8 brooms.
No more than 4 witches can fit on a broom, and no fewer than 2 witches can ride on a broom. Show and explain with pictures, words, and numbers how you would place all 20 witches on 8 brooms.

WHEN TO USE:

After teaching units on addition and subtraction.

WHAT THIS TASK ACCOMPLISHES

It allows students to work with a problem that has several rules to follow as well as multiple solutions. It also gives students a chance to create diagrams, sentences, numbers and equations to communicate their solutions.

CONCEPTS ASSESSED AND SKILLS DEVELOPED

- Problem solving
- Reasoning
- Communication
- Strategy: trial-and-error
- Combinations

WHAT STUDENTS WILL DO

Some students will draw one broom with several witches at a time and guess/predict as they go. Some draw all brooms, then fill each broom with one witch at a time. Others may draw all brooms, place two witches on each, and then place the others. Still others will draw all brooms and then fill each with four witches. They will then scatter the remaining witches or leave off brooms. Finally, some students will fill the brooms with four witches and erase one at a time until they get to twenty.

TIME REQUIRED FOR TASK

30–40 minutes

TEACHING TIPS

As a pre-assessment activity, cut pictures of brooms and witches out of colored paper. In a whole-group lesson, ask individual students to come to the front of the class and create possible broom loads until all combinations are discovered.

POSSIBLE SOLUTIONS

Two brooms with four witches and six brooms with two.

Four brooms with three witches and four brooms with two.

One broom with four witches, two brooms with three witches, and five brooms with two witches

Author: **Cindy Pierce** teaches at the Marion Cross School in Norwich, Vermont.

Name Novice Date

Witches' Troubles

There are 20 witches who need a ride on a broomstick.
There are 8 brooms.
No more than 4 witches can fit on a broom, and no fewer than 2 witches can ride on a broom. Show and explain with pictures, words, and numbers how you would place all 20 witches on 8 brooms.

This student was distracted by the limitation of having a certain number of witches on each broom. She seemed to think the broom would steer better with three witches. She put three witches on each broom until she ran out of witches and was confident that by showing the extra broom without witches meant she had used eight brooms. She counted until she got to twenty.

Name Apprentice Date

Witches' Troubles

There are 20 witches who need a ride on a broomstick.
There are 8 brooms.
No more than 4 witches can fit on a broom, and no fewer than 2 witches can ride on a broom. Show and explain with pictures, words, and numbers how you would place all 20 witches on 8 brooms.

This student missed the idea of using eight brooms. He solved some of the problem by using twenty witches and putting no more than four on a broom. He drew three on a broom and counted the total and then drew four and eventually five witches. His idea that he had no room was true in that there were no more witches to ride on the brooms. He fully grasped that the limit was twenty witches.

Name Practitioner Date

Witches' Troubles

There are 20 witches who need a ride on a broomstick.
There are 8 brooms.
No more than 4 witches can fit on a broom, and no fewer than 2 witches can ride on a broom. Show and explain with pictures, words, and numbers how you would place all 20 witches on 8 brooms.

This student was comfortable with all of the limitations and requirements. She was able to find a solution using a strategy of estimating as she went along until all the brooms were full with appropriate numbers of witches. She was very clear when explaining her solution.

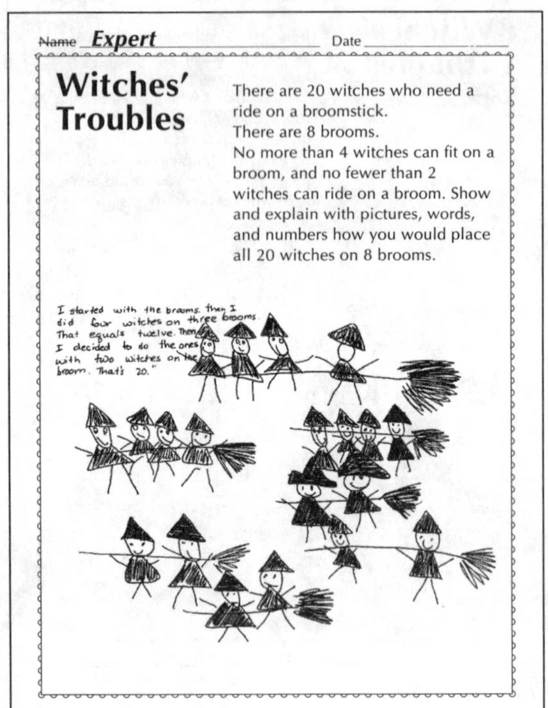

Name *Expert* Date

Witches' Troubles

There are 20 witches who need a ride on a broomstick.
There are 8 brooms.
No more than 4 witches can fit on a broom, and no fewer than 2 witches can ride on a broom. Show and explain with pictures, words, and numbers how you would place all 20 witches on 8 brooms.

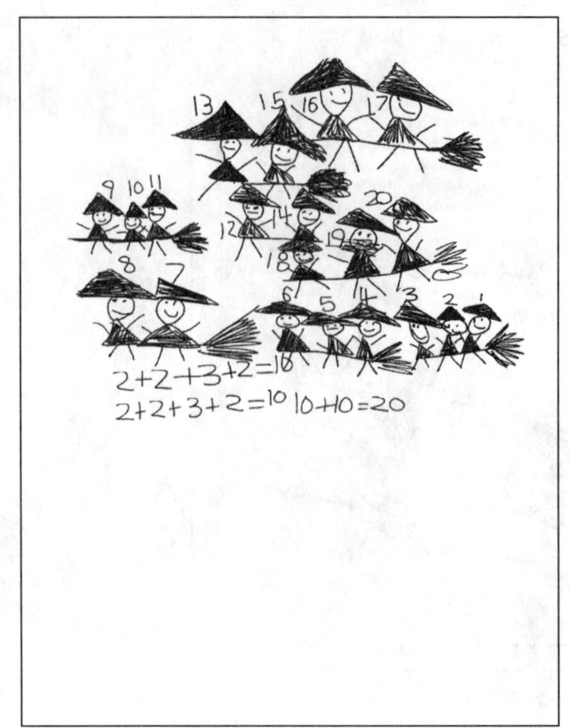

This student has a deep understanding of the problem and was able to find two solutions. She understands that four threes equals twelve and counted by twos to reach one of othe solutions. She was able to represent one of her solutions with an addition equation. She wrote numbers next to each witch to verify her solution. Her explanation involved appropriate use of mathematical terminology and notation.

Name ______________________________ Date ____________________

Shoe Graph

Find three objects to measure in the classroom with your pair of shoes. Choose a pair of shoes from your teacher to measure the same object. What observations and comparisons can you make about the length of the objects that you measured?

Shoe Graph

Teaching Tips Page

Grade Level: K–2

THE TASK

Find three objects to measure in the classroom with your pair of shoes. Choose a pair of shoes from your teacher to measure the same object. What observations and comparisons can you make about the length of the objects that you measured?

WHEN TO USE

After a unit on measurement

WHAT THIS TASK ACCOMPLISHES

It requires children to measure length and width in nonstandard units.

CONCEPTS ASSESSED AND SKILLS DEVELOPED

- Measurement
- Estimation
- Whole number operations
- Patterns and relationships
- Problem solving
- Communication
- Reasoning

WHAT STUDENTS WILL DO

Children choose any three items in the classroom to measure length and width. They will use tally marks and numerical representation along with a sketch of the object. We did take time before the measurement activity began to figure out which shoes belonged to each of my three daughters, which were mine, and which belonged to Mr. Haddock, so that they could label them during the activity.

TIME REQUIRED FOR THE TASK:

About an hour-and-a-half

TEACHING TIPS

Bring in many pairs of larger-size shoes so students can make comparisons.

It is very meaningful for young children to investigate the measurement using their hands, arms, feet, paper clips, yarn, or unifix cubes before being asked to accurately measure with rulers. We also had drawing games by just learning how to hold the ruler straight and how to stop and start on the ruler. Have children trace each other's feet and cut out a pair to decorate. You can incorporate graphing activities with this problem. Finding the area of their foot or hand using inch paper or centimeter paper is also an extension that may be investigated.

Talk about why it is important for everyone to use the same length of measurement. Ask the children to think of jobs in which workers need to make measurements of any kind (shoe salespeople, cooks, postal workers, pharmacists, etc.).

SUGGESTED MATERIALS

- Shoes, string, paper, pencil, manipulatives, other materials for measuring

POSSIBLE SOLUTIONS

The children at the Practitioner and Expert levels should be making accurate comparisons of how their shoe measurements contrast with the larger shoe measurements. They should realize that if they use a larger shoe, it would take more of their own smaller shoe and less of the larger shoe to measure the same objects. They should also be able to estimate (given a variety of shoes) what would happen when they compare measurements. The children would become aware of the patterns of measuring similar-size objects with the same shoes.

Author: **Sandy Haddock** is a first-grade teacher at Bristol Elementary School in Bristol, Vermont.

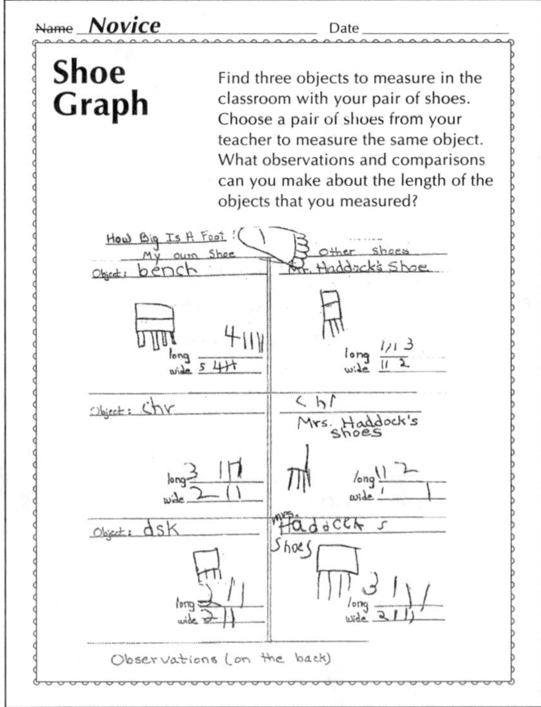

Name *Novice* Date

Shoe Graph

Find three objects to measure in the classroom with your pair of shoes. Choose a pair of shoes from your teacher to measure the same object. What observations and comparisons can you make about the length of the objects that you measured?

How Big Is A Foot?
My own Shoe | Other shoes
Object: bench | Mr. Haddock's Shoe
Object: chr | chr Mrs. Haddock's shoes
Object: dsk | Mrs. Haddcck s Shoes
Observations (on the back)

Dictation
"My shoes are smaller than Mr. Haddocks. It took less of my shoe than Mr. Haddock on the bench. It took more of my shoes on the chair because that number is the highest. I learned about big and small.

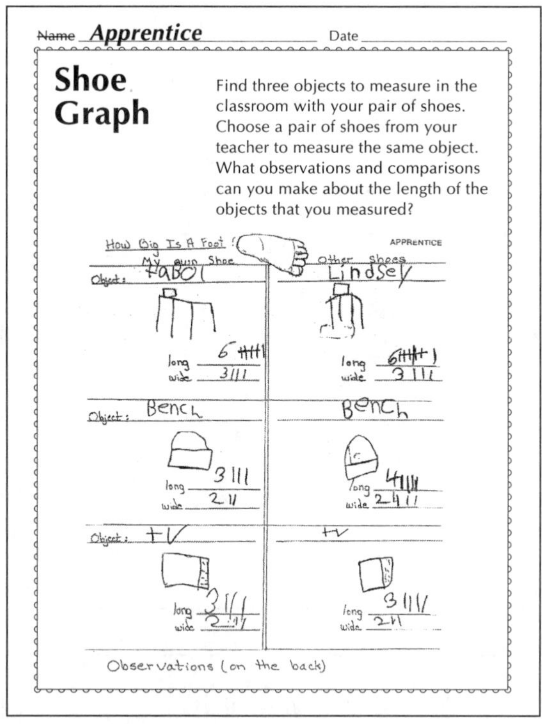

Name *Apprentice* Date

Shoe Graph

Find three objects to measure in the classroom with your pair of shoes. Choose a pair of shoes from your teacher to measure the same object. What observations and comparisons can you make about the length of the objects that you measured?

How Big Is A Foot? APPRENTICE
My own Shoe | Other shoes
Object: TaBOl | Lindsey
Object: Bench | Bench
Object: TV | TV
Observations (on the back)

2+3+3+5+2+2=18 (incorrect equasion)

3+3+5+7+3 = 18 (incorrect equasion)

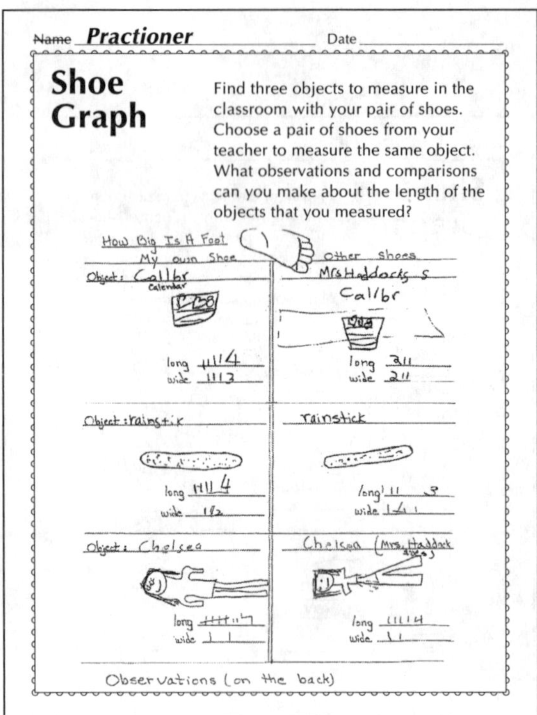

~~Name~~ *Practioner* Date

Shoe Graph

Find three objects to measure in the classroom with your pair of shoes. Choose a pair of shoes from your teacher to measure the same object. What observations and comparisons can you make about the length of the objects that you measured?

How Big Is A Foot

My own Shoe	Other shoes
Object: Callbr (calendar) long ++114 wide 1113	MrsHaddocks Call/br long 311 wide 211
Object: rainstix long ++11 4 wide 1½	rainstick long 11 3 wide 1
Object: Chelsea long ++++11 wide 1 1	Chelsea (Mrs. Haddock shoes) long 1114 wide 1

Observations (on the back)

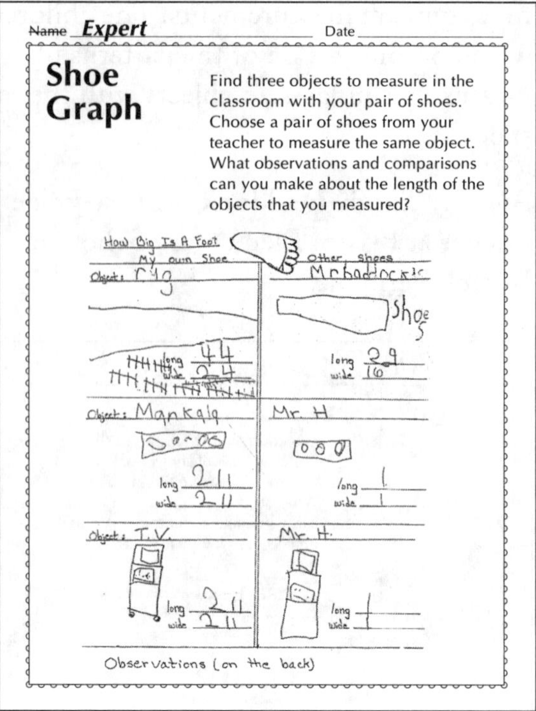

~~Name~~ *Expert* Date

Shoe Graph

Find three objects to measure in the classroom with your pair of shoes. Choose a pair of shoes from your teacher to measure the same object. What observations and comparisons can you make about the length of the objects that you measured?

How Big Is A Foot

My own Shoe	Other shoes
Object: rug long 44 wide 24	Mr haddocks shoes long 29 wide 16
Object: Mankala long 2 1 wide 2 1	Mr. H long 1 wide 1
Object: T.V. long 2 1 wide 2 1	Mr. H. long 1 wide 1

Observations (on the back)

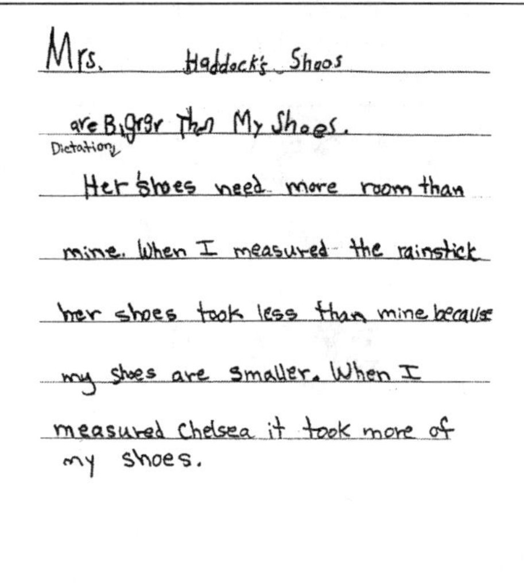

Mrs. Haddock's Shoos are Bigrgr Then My Shoes.

Dictation

Her shoes need more room than mine. When I measured the rainstick her shoes took less than mine because my shoes are smaller. When I measured Chelsea it took more of my shoes.

Dictation

"My number is higher on the rug because my shoes were smaller. Mr. Haddock's shoes are bigger but the number got lesser. On the Mankala and T.V. it was only 1 for Mr. Haddock's shoe. His shoes are still bigger.

What would happen if you used your dad's shoes?

"I think they would be lesser because my dad's shoes are bigger like Mr. Haddocks.

Name ______________________________ Date ____________________

Hamsters

Sam's hamster, Applesauce, had 8 babies. There were 4 males and 4 females. When they were six weeks old, the females each had 6 babies, 3 males and 3 females. This time Sam knew he had to separate them as soon as they were old enough. The pet store told him to put them in separate cages for four weeks. The pet store told him there should be no more than 3 hamsters in each cage. How many cages will Sam need if he wants the females and males in different cages? Show your cages below. Please explain how you got your answer.

Hamsters

Teaching Tips Page

Grade Level: K–2

THE TASK

Sam's hamster, Applesauce, had 8 babies. There were 4 males and 4 females. When they were six weeks old, the females each had 6 babies, 3 males and 3 females. This time Sam knew he had to separate them as soon as they were old enough. The pet store told him to put them in separate cages for four weeks. The pet store told him there should be no more than 3 hamsters in each cage. How many cages will Sam need if he wants the females and males in different cages? Show your cages below. Please explain how you got your answer.

WHEN TO USE

When teaching computation and whole numbers

WHAT THIS TASK ACCOMPLISHES

It assesses students' ability to follow, organize, and solve a multistep problem.

CONCEPTS ASSESSED AND SKILLS DEVELOPED

Whole Number Operations:

- Developing meaning for and sense of operations through problem situations
- Relating math language and symbols of operations to problem situations

Whole Number Computation:

- Selecting and using computation techniques

Spatial Sense:

- Organizing cages and hamsters in a given space

Problem Solving:

- Using problem-solving approaches to investigate and understand mathematical content

Communication:

- Using pictorial, written/verbal, and numerical ways to explain solution

Reasoning:

- Draw logical conclusions

Connections:

- Using past knowledge and experience to solve the problem

WHAT STUDENTS WILL DO

Some students will add up all or some of the numbers on the sheet (8+6=14, 8+4+4+6+3+3=28, and many other varieties). With this total, they will make cages, each of which will hold no more than three hamsters.

Some students will be so engaged in drawing the hamsters that they lose track of the problem and the solution.

Some students will not include Applesauce.

Some students will draw boxes or circles around the symbols to show cages.

Some students will explain with words and/or equations.

Some students will mix males and females while focusing on keeping no more than 3 hamsters in each cage.

Some students will show males and females having babies.

TIME REQUIRED FOR TASK

20–30 minutes

TEACHING TIPS

Encourage students not to do detailed drawings of cages or hamsters.

Brainstorm symbols to show female and male hamsters (m/f, circle/square, x/o, etc....)

Discuss the meaning of "no more than 3 hamsters in a cage" so that it is clear that there could be 1–3 hamsters in a cage.

Discuss the reason behind separating males and females. During this discussion, you may find yourself nervous about the developmental appropriateness of the discussion or where the discussion may lead with certain students. I found the first graders to be very matter-of-fact and surprisingly focused on the problem rather than how those babies got there. They simply stated that when males and females are together, they make more babies.

SUGGESTED MATERIALS

Have available manipulatives for those who may want to use them (colored blocks, unifix cubes, beans, etc.).

POSSIBLE SOLUTIONS

There are 21 possible solutions. There could be 12–33 cages to keep the females separate from the males and to have no more than 3 hamsters in a cage. After all the students had completed the problem, we went over the solutions with 12 cages and 33 cages.

Author: **Cindy Pierce** is a first-grade teacher at the Marion Cross School in Norwich, Vermont.

Name ______________________________ Date ____________________

Pizza Party

Tim and Lisa are having friends over for a pizza party. There will be 5 children, including Lisa and Tim. Each child wants 3 slices of pizza. How many whole pizzas do they need? How will the pizzas be cut into fractional parts?

Pizza Party

Teaching Tips Page

Grade Level: K–2

THE TASK

Tim and Lisa are having friends over for a pizza party. There will be 5 children, including Lisa and Tim. Each child wants 3 slices of pizza. How many whole pizzas do they need? How will the pizzas be cut into fractional parts?

WHEN TO USE

After teaching units on fractions, geometry, patterns, and whole numbers

WHAT THIS TASK ACCOMPLISHES

It is very open-ended, which provides for numerous solutions. The students need to decide what size of slices to give each friend at the pizza party. They also have to keep in mind that there is an equal number of slices for each child. They can use halves, thirds, fourths, or sixths to decide how many slices they want to divide the pizza circles into. This talk challenges their understanding of the concepts of whole, equal, and fractional parts.

CONCEPTS ASSESSED AND SKILLS DEVELOPED

- Fractional parts
- Concepts of whole number operations
- Geometry
- Patterns and relationships
- Problem solving
- Reasoning
- Connections

WHAT STUDENTS WILL DO

The students are provided with a sheet of 2-inch circles and are asked to prepare "pizza orders" for the five friends. They prepare their circles with cheese, sauce, pepperoni, mushrooms, or green peppers. More circles are provided than needed.

The students represent the 5 friends by drawing faces on their paper; they are asked to figure out how many whole pizzas they would need if each friend wanted 3 slices. Then they decide how they will divide the pizza circles into equal fractional slices by folding, cutting, and gluing them near the faces they had previously drawn. The students are encouraged to use the fractional words and/or write fractions to demonstrate their understanding of fractional parts with their written or oral explanations.

TIME REQUIRED FOR TASK

60–75 minutes

TEACHING TIPS

It is important for young children to practice dividing real foods or objects into equal and unequal amounts with partners or cooperative groups to understand the concepts of whole and fractional parts. Before cutting the foods, invite the children to explain how the snack should be divided so that everyone gets the same amount.

Use magazines to select illustrations of foods or favorite scenes that could be divided equally into halves, thirds, or fourths. They can be laminated to be used as puzzle games.

Fraction "hunts": Working in pairs, kids can look all around the classroom and school building for objects that were divided into equal parts such as windows, cabinets, pocket folders, bookcases etc. This was also extended to a family math activity for homework. This may also be extended to nature walks.

Sixths are harder to understand with circles and can be confused with thirds. The students watched demonstrations and practiced helping each other fold and cut circles into 6 equal parts.

Pattern blocks can be used to explore the shapes to find those that are halves, thirds, or sixths of another. If you have an overhead, let the children demonstrate for the classmates how they matched pattern-shaped pieces to the shape.

Link to: Health/Nutrition (preparing healthy fractional snacks & planning a class pizza celebration). Social Studies (researching the origins of pizza). Science (go on nature walks to look for things that have equal parts).

SUGGESTED MATERIALS

- Foods (muffins, bananas, apples, oranges, cookies, graham crackers, chocolate bars, pizza)
- Pattern blocks
- Magazines for fractional picture puzzles
- Pizza (donated boxes and cardboard inserts, real pizza)
- Literature: *Eating Fractions* by Bruce McMillan; *The Half-Birthday Party* by Charlotte Pomerantz; *Each Orange Had 8 Slices* by Paul Giganti, Jr.

POSSIBLE SOLUTIONS

This task is open- ended, and many solutions are possible. Each student will show whether he or she will use halves, thirds, fourths, or sixths in dividing their pizza slices. The reasoning skills and connections that they make will be reflected in showing equal slices and in how they showed or explained leftover parts of pizza.

Author: **Sandy Haddock** teaches grade one at the Bristol Elementary School in Bristol, Vermont.

Name ______________________ Date ______________

Clay Pots

Three Native American Indians made 6 clay pots. Show how many each could have made.

Clay Pots

Teaching Tips Page

Grade Level: K–2

THE TASK

Three Native American Indians made 6 clay pots. Show how many each could have made.

WHEN TO USE

After teaching a unit on addition.

CONCEPTS ASSESSED AND SKILLS DEVELOPED

- Problem solving
- Reasoning and decision making
- Communication
- Number sense
- Additions

WHAT THIS TASK ACCOMPLISHES

The task shows the children's mathematical thinking about combining different numbers in many different ways to equal a given sum. Students will see that there are several solutions/combinations that correctly answer this problem.

WHAT STUDENTS WILL DO

In solving this problem, the student may use manipulative materials to show the different combinations possible to make the pots. They will record the finding through drawings/ writings and numerical equations. Students may find only one or numerous solutions. The number of correct solutions and the explanation of them will determine the level of performance.

TIME REQUIRED FOR THE TASK

Children will need varying amounts of time, and the number of solutions found will also vary depending on the maturity, confidence and developmental level of the individual. During a conference/share time, the teacher will be able to decide which factor(s) may interfere with or enhance their performance.

TEACHING TIPS

Students should be encouraged to explore a variety of solutions.

Students should be allowed to select manipulative and writing/drawing supplies they are comfortable with and motivated by.

A lot of paper should be available so students can self-correct and edit their work.

Students need to have had previous opportunities to work on and share multiple answer problems.

Students need to explain/defend their solutions in a variety of ways—writing, drawing and telling.

SUGGESTED MATERIALS

A variety of manipulative materials

Pictures of Native Americans and their pottery

Writing/coloring utensils

Several sheets of plain paper per person

POSSIBLE SOLUTIONS

6+0+0	3+3+0
5+1+0	3+2+1
4+2+0	2+2+2
4+1+1	

Children may have 1+3+2 and 1+2+3 as well as 3+1+2. All are acceptable as separate solutions at this level.

Author: **Linda Lamb** is a primary-grade teacher in Gwinnett County Public Schools in Georgia.

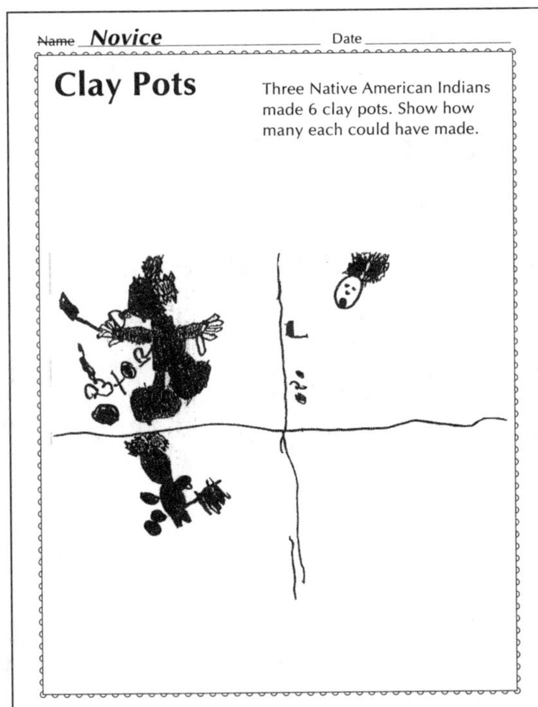

This student is unable to apply the problem-solving process to this situation. A drawing or words may be present, but they are not related to a solution or in defense of explanation of an idea.

This student displays an understanding of putting numbers together to get a solution. Some equations are incomplete and/or inaccurate. A solution is found, but there is a random or weak explanation of strategy.

Name **Practitioner** Date

Clay Pots

Three Native American Indians made 6 clay pots. Show how many each could have made.

2+2+2=6

3+3=6

4x2=6

1+7=6

This student understands the problem and used the appropriate equation. Has one correct solution. The student can communicate/describe the strategy used to solve the problem.

This student has more than one solution, and used an appropriate equation for each. The student can explain the difference between the solutions as well as the process or strategy for each solution. Gives elaborated discussion on process(es).

Name ______________________________ Date ____________________

Reading for Mom

Your mother has you read every evening except Sundays, for 15 minutes. Show how much time you spend reading in the evenings every week.

Reading for Mom

Teaching Tips Page

Grade Level: K–2

THE TASK

Your mother has you read every evening except Sundays, for 15 minutes. Show how much time you spend reading in the evenings every week.

WHEN TO USE

After teaching a unit on addition

WHAT THIS TASK ACCOMPLISHES

Students learn to integrate problem solving, time, number sense and computation. Students also manipulate numbers, demonstrating their number sense and computational abilities.

CONCEPTS ASSESSED AND SKILLS DEVELOPED

- Problem solving
- Reasoning
- Communication
- Number sense
- Addition

WHAT STUDENTS WILL DO

Students will determine that there are six days when they will read for 15 minutes and combine six 15s to arrive at 90 total minutes.

TIME REQUIRED FOR THE TASK

30 minutes

SUGGESTED MATERIALS

- Paper and pencil
- Manipulatives to represent units of time

POSSIBLE SOLUTIONS

90 minutes

1 1/2 hours

1 hour and 30 minutes

Author: **Sandy Hicks** is a veteran of 27 years in the classroom, having taught K–3. Currently she is teaching second grade at Broadway Elementary in Grand Junction, Colorado.

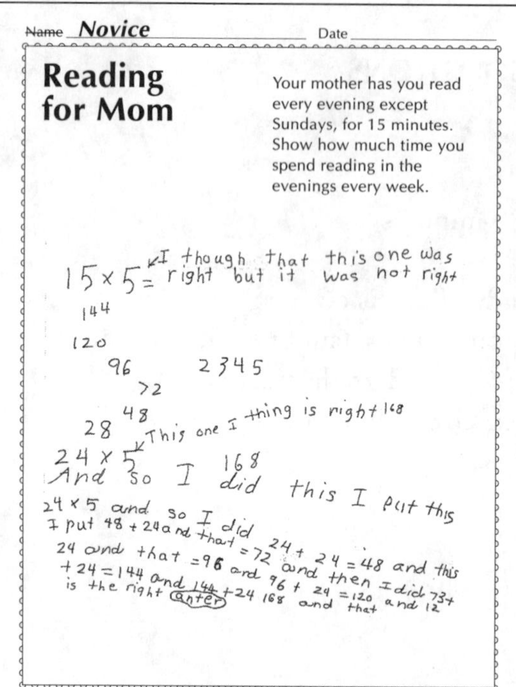

This student actually tries to start the problem and makes a promising beginning by multiplying 15 X 5, indicating that there may be a rudimentary understanding of the problem. However, s/he very quickly loses control, and it seems there is no understanding. Beyond 15 X 5, there is no apparent strategy. The attempt to communicate is confused.

This student has an understanding of what needs to be done: The amount of time spent reading is multiplied by the number of days. However, the use of 60, instead of 15 minutes, and the total of 300 minutes a day indicates that the student did not fully understand the problem. There is also a computation error—the correct total is 360. There is no explanation of the student's thinking.

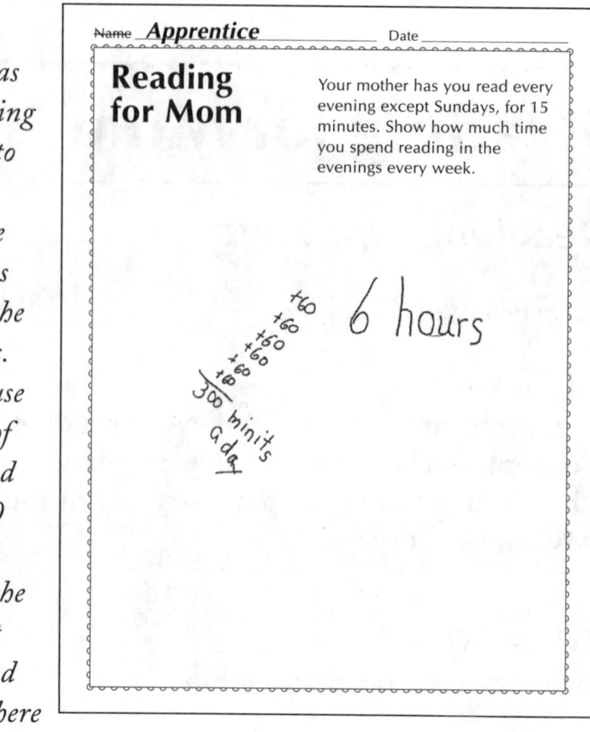

The Expert's solutions contained extensions, like showing why one would need six 15s. He had detailed explanations in mathematical terms and/or number equations showing the solutions to the problem. The student indicated that 7 days minus 1 equals 6 days. There is a formula as well as a verbal explanation.

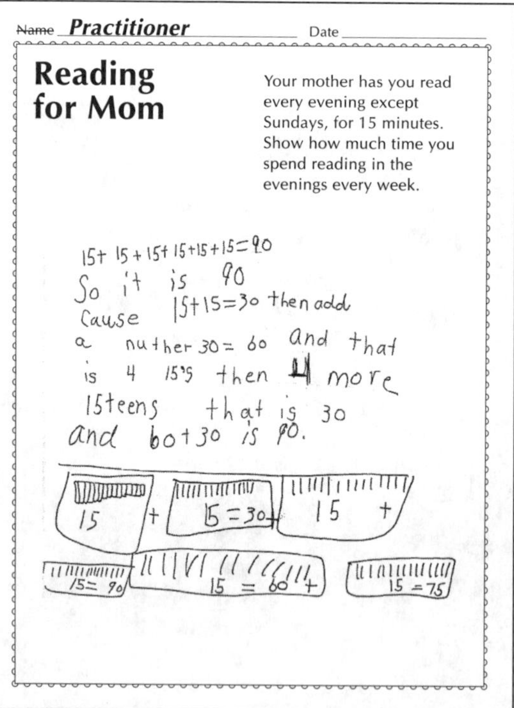

This student added six 15s. The student had a clear understanding of the problem and a strategy that led to a solution. She used words or number equations to explain the task, and used a diagram to help her solve the problem.

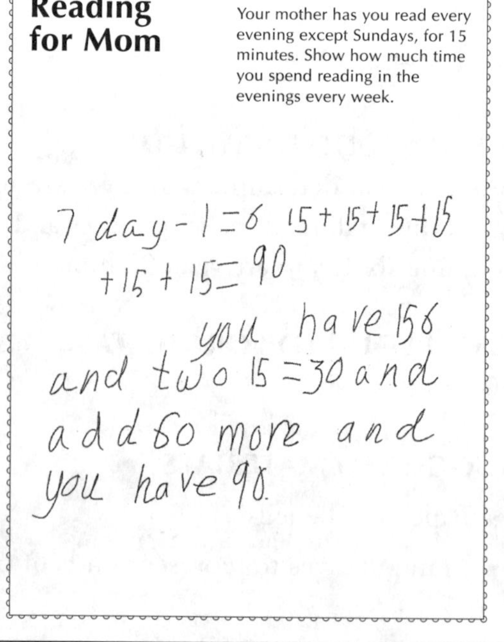

Name ______________________________ Date ____________________

Problem-Solving Form

UNDERSTAND: What is the challenge? ____________________

____

____

PLAN: What did you think about before solving it (clues, past learning, ideas, steps, equations)?

____

____

____

____

SOLVE (and resolve): What strategies did you try?

____

____

____

Describe your best strategy. (You may star a strategy from above.)

____

____

____

____

Name ______________________ Date ______________

Problem-Solving Form (page 2)

LOOK BACK/LOOK FORWARD:

How did you check your solutions?

____

____

____

How did you share your ideas and solutions (charts, drawings, talking, video, maps, etc.)?

____

____

____

What did you learn (general rules, better ways to do things)?

____

____

____

How can you use what you've learned in the future?

____

____

____

____

Name____________________ Date____________

ASSESSMENT OF STUDENT THINKING: A Planning Grid

	Problem Solving	Reasoning	Communication	Statistics and Probability	Geometry and Spatial Sense	Fractions
Standardized achievement subtests						
Matrix sampling						
NAEP/state tests						
Teacher-made criterion-referenced tests						
Teacher observation						
Journals/writing samples						
Checklists						
Interviews						
Exhibitions						
Inventories						
Portfolios of student work						
Child study anecdotal records						
Extended projects						
Critical incidents						
Other						
Columns across top of grid						
Problem solving						
Reasoning						
Communication						
Statistics and probability						
Geometry and spatial sense						
Fractions						

Name ________________________________ Date ____________________

Student Reflection Form

Why I chose this math problem for my portfolio: ____________

____

____

____

____

____

What I learned about myself as a mathematician from doing this math problem: ______________________________

____

____

____

____

How I think I can improve as a mathematician: ____________

____

____

____

____

____

EXEMPLARS RUBRIC

Level	Understanding	Strategies, Reasoning, Procedures	Communication
Novice	• There is no solution, or the solution has no relationship to the task. • Inappropriate concepts or procedures are used.	• No evidence of a strategy or procedure, or uses a strategy that does not help solve the problem. • No evidence of mathematical reasoning. • There were so many errors in mathematical procedure that the problem could not be solved.	• There is no explanation of the solution, the explanation cannot be understood or it is unrelated to the problem. • There is no use or inappropriate use of mathematical representations (e.g., figures, diagrams, graphs, tables, etc.) • There is no use, or mostly inappropriate use, of mathematical terminology and notation.
Apprentice	• The solution is not complete, indicating that parts of the problem are not understood.	• Uses a strategy that is partially useful, leading some way toward a solution, but not to a full solution of the problem. • Some evidence of mathematical reasoning. • Could not completely carry out mathematical procedures.	• There is an incomplete explanation; it may not be clearly presented. • There is some use of appropriate mathematical representation. • There is some use of mathematical terminology and notation appropriate to the problem.
Practitioner	• The solution shows that the student has a broad understanding of the problem and the major concepts necessary for its solution.	• Uses a strategy that leads to a solution of the problem. • Uses effective mathematical reasoning. • Mathematical procedures used appropriately.	• There is a clear explanation. • There is appropriate use of accurate mathematical representation. • There is effective use of mathematical terminology and notation.
Expert	• The solution shows a deep understanding of the problem, including the ability to identify the appropriate mathematical concepts and the information necessary for its solution.	• Uses a very efficient and sophisticated strategy leading directly to a solution. • Employs refined and complex reasoning. • Applies procedures accurately to correctly solve the problem and verify the results.	• There is a clear, effective explanation detailing how the problem is solved. All of the steps are included so that the reader does not need to infer how and why decisions were made. • Mathematical representation is actively used as a means of communicating ideas related to the solution of the problem. • There is precise and appropriate use of mathematical terminology and notation.

How to Assess Problem-Solving Skills in Math by Bena Kallick and Ross Brewer,Scholastic Professional Books, 1997

MATH STUDENT RUBRIC

Level	Understanding	Strategies, Reasoning, Procedures	Communication
Novice	I do not understand the problem.	I am not sure how to do it.	I have no explanation. I'm not sure how to draw the problem, or which numbers to use.
Apprentice	I think I understand the problem.	I got started. I'm still thinking. I have part of the answer. It would help me to work with somebody.	I can explain some of what I did. I tried to use pictures, numbers, graphs, or words. My answer might be right.
Practitioner	I got it! I understand the problem.	I used a plan to solve the problem.	I can tell you or show you how I got the answer. I used mathematical terms and models, pictures, graphs, or numbers to explain how I did the problem. You can see how I did it.
Expert	I got it! I can prove to you that I'm right. I know I'm right.	I can show you several plans to solve this problem. I can prove to you that my answer is right.	I very clearly laid out step by step how I solved the problem. I used words, pictures, numbers, models, or graphs to show exactly how I did the problem, and proved that my answer is right. I can even show you another way to do the problem.

How to Assess Problem-Solving Skills in Math by Bena Kallick and Ross Brewer,Scholastic Professional Books, 1997

Exemplars was formed in 1992 to meet the needs of teachers, curriculum coordinators, and administrators implementing authentic performance assessment in their schools. Exemplars works with a national network of educators to create challenging, real-world mathematics and science problems appropriate for a range of ages and abilities. Exemplars distributes the problems to subscribers along with scoring rubrics keyed to the NCTM Standards, student benchmark papers, and instructional tips to help teachers introduce problem solving to their students.

For more information, contact:

Exemplars
271 Poker Hill Road
Underhill, VT 05489
(800) 450-4050
E-mail: exemplar@sover.net
Web page: www.exemplars.com

Technology Pathways integrates the best uses of technology to provide curriculum, instruction, and assessment pathways for improving student performance. To order a CD-ROM that includes 180 math tasks, benchmark student work, scoring procedures, tools for planning and grading, as well as staff development material for teachers, contact:

Technology Pathways
12 Crooked Mile Road
Westport, CT 06880
(203) 457-9089
E-mail: Hunsickerc@aol.com

Notes

Notes

Notes

Notes

Notes

Notes

Notes

Name ______________________ Date ______________

Muffins

Muffins cost 25¢. How many ways can you pay for the muffin?
Please show and explain your work using pictures, numbers, and words.